Getting Started in
Prints and Patterns

Books in the *Getting Started* series

Getting Started in
Prints and Patterns

Stanley Rice

The Bruce Publishing Company / New York

Collier-Macmillan Limited / London

CONTENTS

INTRODUCTION

A pattern is anything that occurs more than once in the same way. The world is made up of patterns: the forest has a tree pattern, the tree has a branch pattern, the branch a leaf pattern, and the leaf a cell pattern. The patterns become smaller and smaller. In fact, everything in nature consists of simple atomic patterns that are so small they can be seen only with the most powerful microscopes. Although we are not going to deal with the scientific aspects of pattern, it is worth noting that patterns are not just fancy applied decorations, but rather the basis of everything in nature (Figure 2).

Two types of patterns are visible to the human eye: the *unique* type, such as a fingerprint (Figure 3) or a voiceprint (Figure 4), that does not seem to repeat itself in any way; and the *repeating* pattern, such as that made by the windows of a skyscraper or by the millions of carbon atoms in the graphite of a lead pencil (Figure 5). While this book will be concerned primarily with repeating patterns, unique patterns will also be covered. The unique patterns, like fingerprints, we will call *prints;* the repeating patterns we will simply call *repeating patterns.* Whatever it is that repeats itself we refer to as *the repeat.*

FIGURE 1 Simple potato pattern.

Snowflake

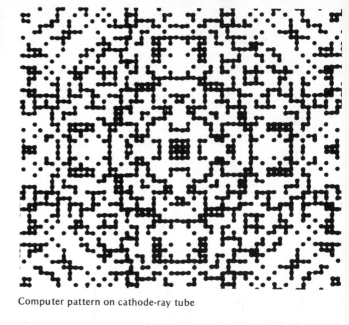
Computer pattern on cathode-ray tube

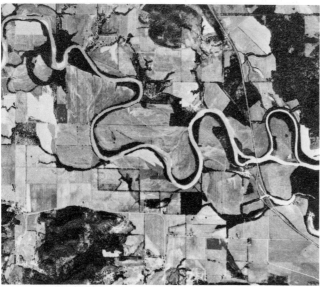
Air photo of Mississippi River   Official U.S. Air Force Photo

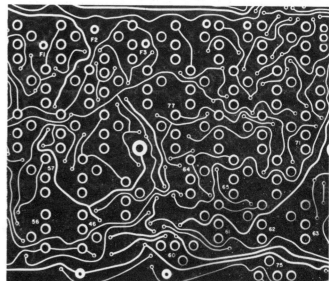
Electronic circuit board

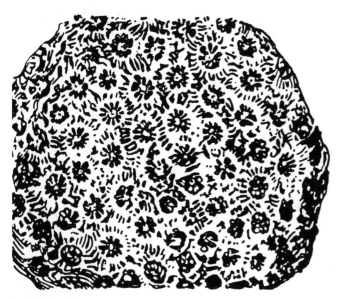
Invertebrate fossils

Patterned textiles   Rug from the Metropolitan
Museum of Art, New York

FIGURE 2   Various natural and artificial patterns.

Man-made repeating patterns are as old as civilization itself, probably having originated from the craftsman's imitation of such things as the weaves in baskets or cloth, and the letters, signs, and symbols used by priests and scribes. Writing itself is the repetition of a limited number of designs called letters, used in various combinations. The page you are reading is a unique pattern.

The patterns you make can be as easy and casual or as difficult and complex as you like. The design in Figure 1 is a simple potato print. Although this book will concentrate only on basic principles that can be put to immediate use, there is no end to the study of pattern if it interests you. Some of the references listed on page 83 explore the more advanced aspects of pattern.

Quantity reproduction processes are not our concern because they can be easily investigated elsewhere. The primary aim of this book is to help you understand how patterns grow and to enable you to sketch and print them easily. When you can do this, you can create your own patterns—patterns that will express you.

Books about printed patterns are often full of complex designs (Figure 6) done by expert artists, sometimes with the help of other craftsmen or machines that are not ordinarily available to most of us. Looking at such work can be rather discouraging and mystifying. This book will try to take some of the mystery out of the subject. We will concentrate on simple tools, materials, and methods and we will use simple examples that you can produce yourself. Bear in mind that good design need not be complicated, and complicated design is not always good.

Naturalistic or realistic drawing is not very important in pattern work. Drawing is unnecessary because the pattern method is itself so extraordinary. With your help, patterns will "grow" in regular ways, seemingly with a life of their own. What can be done just by repeating shapes, colors, and textures has enabled many people who were not professional artists to do pattern work that is so satisfying and beautiful that it is collected by museums throughout the world. The method does much of the work; it is the message. In fact, almost any shape can make a good-looking pattern if you repeat it in the right way.

FIGURE 3 Fingerprint.

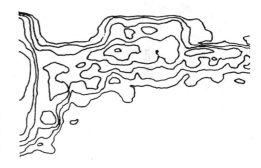

FIGURE 4 Voiceprint of the word *you*.

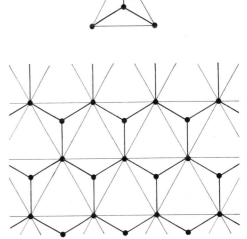

FIGURE 5 Carbon atoms in the graphite of a lead pencil.

FIGURE 6   Wallpaper design by William Morris.

Courtesy of the Cooper-Hewitt Museum of Design,
The Smithsonian Institution

1

BASIC SHAPES AND SKETCHES

Patterns cover the surfaces of everything from buildings to candy wrappers. They can be used on the outside of three-dimensional objects as well as on flat surfaces. You can even make three-dimensional patterns like those made with plastic or aluminum structural toys. In this book, however, we will describe mainly flat, two-dimensional patterns on paper or cloth. You can always add a dimension by folding the paper or draping the cloth; but you should decide beforehand to which of these uses the flat pattern will be put, and plan the pattern accordingly.

You need not cover a flat surface completely with pattern or color for the cloth or paper itself can be part of the pattern. The extent of the area to be covered is up to you. Your paper or cloth can be almost any color, but if you can't find the color you want, dye the paper or cloth yourself. You can even dye it in patterns, as you will see.

SOME BASIC SHAPES

Whether you want to cover a surface completely or partially, it is important to understand the basic shapes that can be repeated and how they work.

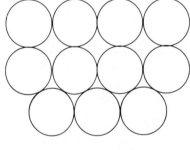

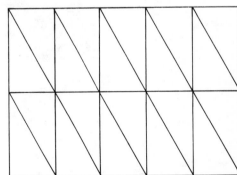

FIGURE 7   Above: circle pattern;
below: rectangle-and-triangle pattern.

1

FIGURE 8 Pattern made
with rectangular cards.

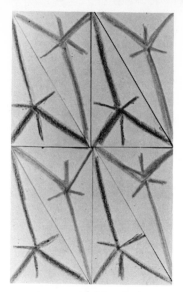

FIGURE 9 Pattern made with
triangular card sections.

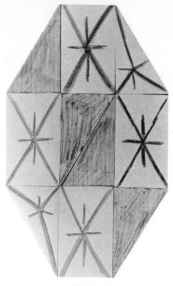

FIGURE 10 Rectangular and
triangular cards.

Try covering any flat surface with coins or checkers. You'll find you can't completely cover any surface with circles of any size unless you put one on top of another; there are always gaps between them (Figure 7). On the other hand, there are many ways in which you can cover a surface with rectangles and triangles without overlaps or gaps (Figure 7). Try it. Take 15 to 20 filing cards and on one side color half of them red and half of them blue. Then cut four red and four blue sections diagonally, making eight triangles of each color. With these cards see what patterns you can make without overlapping the cards or leaving gaps between them.

Turn all the rectangular and triangular cards over and draw red or blue lines from each corner into the middle of each shape, as shown in Figures 8 and 9. Try making patterns with the cards, first using only the second sides and then using either side. Many kinds of patterns are possible (Figures 9 and 10).

POTATO PRINTING

Try making some patterns of your own. It's easy to get started with only some plain white paper, a small potato (new potatoes are best), a foam-rubber stamp pad and a penknife (Figure 11). If you don't have a stamp pad, substitute some colored ink and a small ink dabber of foam rubber or folded cloth. Or use poster color and a flat paintbrush about one inch wide to "ink" the potato for printing. Don't worry about careful planning at this stage. It is more important to make some patterns by experimenting and to experience mistakes.

FIGURE 11 Equipment for
a simple potato pattern.

To obtain two printing surfaces, make a very straight cut through the potato with a sharp knife. This may take a little practice because the printing surfaces have to be as flat and smooth as possible. With a penknife, cut into one of the printing surfaces, leaving a raised, or relief, design — cut a star, a moon, or any other design you wish. Then stamp, dab, or brush some ink or poster color onto the design you have cut, and stamp it on the paper to create a pattern. This pattern can be designed in one of three ways: you can apply the design in a random manner; make a formal pattern of rows (Figures 12 and 13), columns, or circles which will look geometrical and regular; or make a representational pattern that looks like a particular object (for instance, many leaf shapes resemble trees). After deciding on the method you prefer, keep adding color to the potato and stamping until your pattern is completed.

Whatever design method you choose, your repeating pattern is usually made up of two parts: the structure or framework of the pattern and the design that is put into the framework. The framework is a formal structure, like an empty house, bookshelf, or picture frame; anything can be put into it. In potato printing the oval shape of the potato is the individual unit of the framework and the design is cut within this unit. To make a repeating rather than a unique pattern, first choose a structure for the repeating units. Then it is easier to decide what to put into the structure. First the structure and then the design.

FIGURE 12   Formal potato pattern.

FIGURE 13   Rough potato print.

GUM-ERASER PRINTING

Gum-eraser printing is essentially the same as potato printing; it merely substitutes an eraser for the potato. Both methods can be used to make final patterns (Plate 1), but they are most often used in making preliminary rough printings or sketches of the pattern. Being able to sketch patterns easily is useful, for it helps you to visualize the final design and enables you to practice the procedure involved.

Gather the following materials that are shown in Figure 14; they can all be purchased at a dime store:

Half dozen art gum erasers (1 x 1 x 2 inches)

Foam-rubber stamp pad (red is a cheerful color to get)

An extra bottle of stamp-pad ink

Square graph paper with heavy one-inch divisions

Plain paper (8½ x 11 inches)

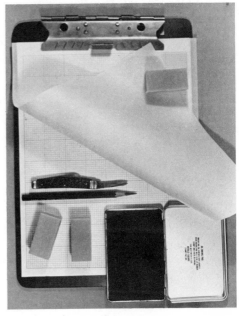

FIGURE 14   Equipment for gum-eraser printing.

BASIC SHAPES AND SKETCHES

Tracing paper or thin bond (8½ x 11 inches)

Penknife

Clipboard

The sides and ends of the erasers are rectangles or squares that you can use as printing surfaces with which to make patterns. First put a sheet of tracing paper over a sheet of graph paper and attach them both to the clipboard, with some extra plain paper underneath for padding. Using the erasers with the stamp pad, try making various patterns similar to the ones in Figure 15.

Next take a knife and make some cuts in one end and one side of the eraser. Don't worry about what kind of gouges they are — just take care not to gouge yourself. Print some more patterns, using the gouged surfaces. Make the same pattern you made with the uncut surfaces. The result will not be as regular as the first pattern because of the cuts in the erasers. The first few repeats may not look very impressive, but the more repeats you make, the better the pat-

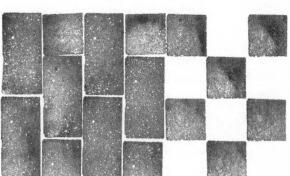

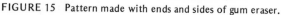

FIGURE 15 Pattern made with ends and sides of gum eraser.

tern will look. If you turn the eraser whenever you print a repeat you will get still more interesting effects.

If you have not already made a checkerboard pattern, try one. It can resemble a real checkerboard, but it doesn't have to be exact to be called a checkerboard pattern. Instead of being empty, each square can have a design in it. That design doesn't have to fill the square or even adjust to it in any obvious way. For example, if you cut a tree into one end of a gum eraser and then print it in a checkerboard (Figure 16), you can still get a variety of patterns depending on how you turn the tree when you print it; they are all still basically checkerboard in structure.

You can also remove the square. Your pattern will then show only the trees without the square checkerboard framework (Figure 16). This is what often happens to the geometrical structure of patterns — you don't see the framework because it has been dropped or "lost." You can design countless patterns using only squares and rectangles and they need not show the frames.

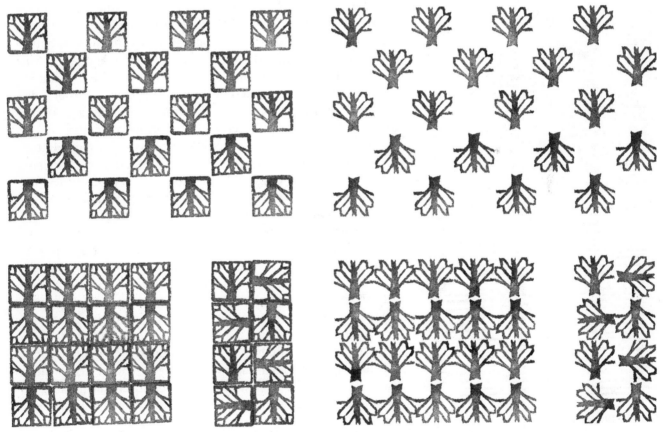

FIGURE 16   Checkerboard gum-eraser patterns with and without frameworks.

BASIC SHAPES AND SKETCHES

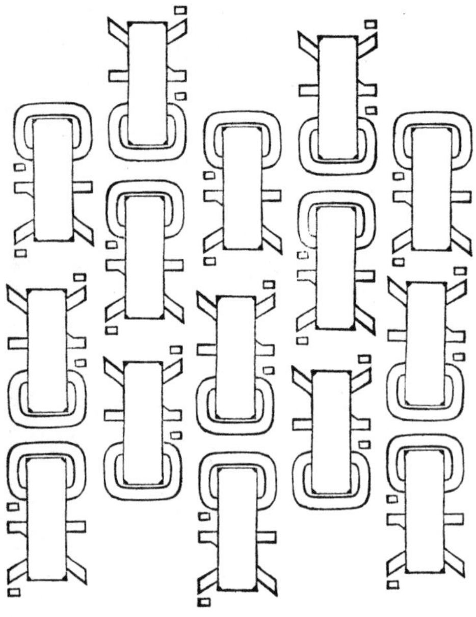

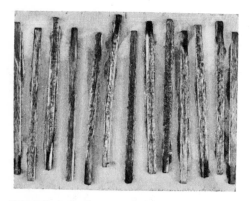
FIGURE 17   O.K. stamp pattern.

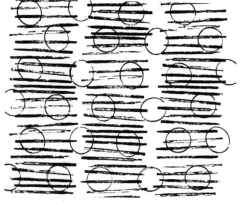
FIGURE 18   Matchsticks glued to a wooden block.

FIGURE 19   Matchstick pattern.

MISCELLANEOUS PRINTING SURFACES

Ordinary items such as a rubber stamp which reads PAID or OK can be interesting when they are printed as patterns (Figure 17). Get a rubber stamp or office stamp at any stationery store and use the materials listed on pages 3-4.

You can peel the message from the stamp and attach the stamp to something else if you wish. Anything that is flat and will take ink from the stamp pad can be used. For temporary use, paste shapes or letters to the base with rubber cement; for more permanent stick, use Elmer's Glue-All. Of course, you can stamp almost any piece of wood that has a flat surface in the same way and you can cut patterns in the surface with a knife. The plank or side grain (cut from the length of the tree trunk, not across the end of it) is the easiest to work with a knife; sometimes the end grain can be used, but it must be cut with an engraver's tool.

Try gluing matchsticks (Figure 18), or cardboard cut into shapes to a smooth wooden block. The rectangular shape of the block is the basic shape or framework into which you put your design (Figure 19). You can also do a lot with plastic letters (Figure 20), which are available at the dime store. Attach them to a small block with rubber cement. Place them in one corner of the block so you will know exactly where they are when the block is upside down and ready for printing (Figure 20). Many letters such as A, Y, H, X, and V are symmetrical in shape and you can print with either side of these. With the other letters, however, you will have to ink the back of the plastic letter so that it prints correctly.

Some of the oldest patterns were developed from letter forms and words. Because combinations of letters have meaning for us, making patterns with letters offers possibilities for communication that are not present with other images. Your initials or some other combination may appeal to you. Try making a pattern with one letter as shown in Figure 21. Patterns made with letters can resemble poems that are meant to be looked at rather than read. Such poems form a branch of modern poetry called "concrete poetry" that explores the way arrangements of letters look in relation to their meaning. What kind of a "yes" do you think is suggested by the typewritten pattern in Figure 22? As you can see, all the letters of the typewritten alphabet fit into the same rectangular shape provided by the metal hammers of the typewriter on which they are mounted. Typewriters are good mechanical pattern-producers as long as the pattern you want is made up of rows of rectangles within which the only images are letters.

GETTING STARTED IN PRINTS AND PATTERNS

FIGURE 20 Plastic letters.

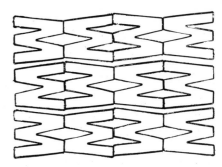

FIGURE 21 Pattern made with one letter.

```
YYYYYYYYYYYYYYYYYYYYYYYYYYYYYYYYYYYYYYYYEEEEEEEEEEEEEEEEEEEEEEEEEEEEESSSSSSSSSSSSSSSSSSSSSSSS
YYYYY       YYYYYYYYYYYYY       YY                          EESSSS            SSSSSSS
YYYYY       YYYYYYYYYYYYY       YY       EEEEEEE       EESS  SSSSSSSSS          SSSSS
YYYYYYY     YYYYYYYYYYYYY      YYYYEE    EEEEEEE       EE  SSSSSSSSSSS          SSSSS
YYYYYYYYY     YYYYYYYYY       YYYYYYEE   EEEEEEEEEEEEEEEE  SSSSSSSSSSSSSSSSSSSSSSSSSSS
YYYYYYYYYYY     YYYYYY        YYYYYYYYEE  EEEEEEEEEEEEEEEE  SSSSSSSSSSSSSSSSSSSSSSSSSSS
YYYYYYYYYYYYY     YY         YYYYYYYYYYEE  EEEE    EEEEEEE    SSSSSSSSSSSSSSSSSSSSSSSS
YYYYYYYYYYYYYY              YYYYYYYYYYYYEE           EEEEEEE          SSSSSSSS
YYYYYYYYYYYYYYY            YYYYYYYYYYYYYEE  EEEE    EEEEEEEESS          SSSSSSS
YYYYYYYYYYYYYYY            YYYYYYYYYYYYYEE  EEEE    EEEEEEEESSSS          SSSSS
YYYYYYYYYYYYYYY            YYYYYYYYYYYYYEE  EEEEEEEEEEEEEEEESSSSSSSSSSSSSSSSSS  SSSSS
YYYYYYYYYYYYYYY            YYYYYYYYYYYYYEE  EEEEEEEEEEEEEEEESSSSSSSSSSSSSSSSSS  SSSSS
YYYYYYYYYYYYYYY            YYYYYYYYYYYYYEE  EEEEEEEEEEEEEEEE     SSSSSSSSSSS  SSSSS
YYYYYYYYYYYYYYY            YYYYYYYYYYYYYEE  EEEEEEE    EE    SSSSSSSSSSS  SSSSS
YYYYYYYYYYYY              YYYYYYYYY       EEEEEEE    EESS   SSSSSSS  SSSSSS
YYYYYYYYYYYY              YYYYYYYYY                 EESSS           SSSSSSSS
YYYYYYYYYYYYYYYYYYYYYYYYYYYYYYYYYYYYYEEEEEEEEEEEEEEEEEEEEEEEEEEESSSSSSSSSSSSSSSSSSSSSSSSS
```

FIGURE 22 Typewritten *yes* pattern.

REGISTERING HANDPRINTED PATTERNS

Chances are that your matchstick blocks, plastic letters, and potatoes do not fit your graph paper as well as the gum erasers do. If they don't, you are encountering a common problem in printing patterns by hand — that of how to keep things regular or in line. Remember that you are not a machine. When you make handprinted patterns the results need not be mechanically perfect. So often the results of a machine's perfection tend to be boring and we find more life and interest in the imperfect products of people. Nevertheless, you will want to be careful when doing a final pattern printing. Here are some points to remember:

1. Don't try to cover a large surface with small repeats unless you use guidelines of some sort.

BASIC SHAPES AND SKETCHES

2. In the sketch stage, use graph paper for your guidelines whenever you can. This is particularly useful when you are printing with gum erasers. Sketching in this medium can save a lot of time, trouble, and exasperation.

3. Work out your larger designs by making a rough sketch on graph paper first. The sketch need not show all the details, but it will enable you to see how the repeating masses and voids look. The graph paper also provides an easy means of enlarging the design. Simply transfer it part by part onto a larger block that is ruled into divisions similar to those on the graph paper (Figure 23).

4. When you sketch or print patterns, apply the repeats systematically so that the design is built up in a regular way. Systematic printing makes it easier to keep the pattern in line and to see the nature of the pattern itself.

FIGURE 23   Graph paper sketch with enlarged design.

5. If you use a general purpose printing block on which to paste designs (Figure 24), use one corner as a registry corner and mark it on the back. If you don't follow this suggestion, you may misregister the block by lining it up on the wrong corner.

6. When you are printing something with difficult registry, it is very easy to get the repeats slightly out of position. Bend down almost level with the block and peek under it as you put it down to see exactly where the block will print. Once you have put it down, of course, do not try to move it.

These are some of the considerations to keep in mind when you are doing careful printing. It is not necessary, however, to be too neat until you get ready to print something important that you will want to keep.

FIGURE 24 Letter attached to one corner of printing block to facilitate correct registry.

PROJECT 1 MATCHBOX

There are many kinds of matchboxes, most of which are easy to cover. The pattern on the box in Figure 25 is a variation of the diamond pattern, and like all diamond patterns it is derived from crossed stripes or lines. The stripes can be crossed at any angle you like. For variety, two little triangles were cut out of one end of the diamond and then added to the outside of the other end.

Because the basic unit was too small to print one at a time, four diamonds were drawn and cut on one 1 x 2 inch eraser block. Measure the area to be covered and then make more than enough pattern. Don't forget that the striking surface is left uncovered. Rule the dimensions of the box on transparent paper first and then put the paper over the pattern so that you can see how the edges of the box relate to the repeat units of the pattern. Score the folds with a paper clip, attach the paper with paste or rubber cement, and spray the covered box with a protective spray. As long as the striking surface lasts, you can put new matches in your box.

FIGURE 25 Covered matchbox.

2

SIMPLE PRINTING METHODS

There are many printing methods available for both repeating and unique patterns. We will concentrate on the simpler methods that are especially suited to sketching and printing designs. These simple methods allow the designer to see exactly what he is doing so that he can make active judgments at every phase of the work's progress. A number of traditional printing techniques will therefore be eliminated, but the advantages gained by this simplification are numerous.

PRINTING SURFACES

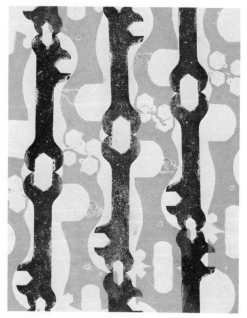

FIGURE 26   Pattern made with wrenches.

Printing surfaces are those that are used to transfer ink or paint to the paper. Both the potato and the gum eraser that were discussed in Chapter 1 are printing surfaces. There are two kinds of printing surfaces: those that are made for the express purpose of printing, and those that can be adapted for printing. The first category, available in art or professional supply stores, includes surfaces made for professional printing use. Among these are ready-made linoleum blocks, plank-grain or end-grain wood used with type, type itself, typographic blanking material, zinc or copper plates, lithographic stones, stencils, and silk screens. You might want to try some of these surfaces on your own, but our concern here will be with the second category — surfaces that can be adapted for printing.

Like potatoes or gum erasers, any surface that will accept pigment and then transfer most of it during the impressing or printing process can be adapted for printing. Floor linoleum, plank pine wood, rubber, glass, steel, sticks, leaves, feathers, various plastics, and many other materials can be adapted (see Figures 26 through 30). Some are useful and easy to work with for many purposes. Others are useful only in special cases, but it is important to know what possibilities are available. The most useful simple printing surfaces are generally flat and smooth. Although it is possible to print from curved surfaces such as cylinders (used in most mechanized printing), such surfaces are generally not suitable for our needs. Potatoes, gum erasers (see Chapter 1), linoleum, and wood will be our most useful printing surfaces, although these materials also have their limitations:

Potatoes — useful for sketch printing, but do not last very long and don't take oil inks very well.

FIGURE 27 Pattern made with gum-rubber erasers.

Gum erasers (Figure 31) — also useful for sketch printing and small jobs; but usually small and rather delicate, and thus impractical for any large-scale printing jobs.

Wood (Figures 32, 33, and 34) — material originally used in block printing. Soft, smooth-grained woods such as pine (the least expensive) and pear are usually used for cutting, which is done on the plank or side grain; if the cross grain of maple or boxwood is used, wood must be engraved. The inherent side-grain wood pattern can be used to advantage when making designs, but the side-grain wood is often difficult to make smooth enough to print solid tones well.

Linoleum — useful for printing large, flat areas of color, since it is relatively soft and has no grain, is easy to cut in any direction (Figure 35). Because of linoleum's relative thinness, however, it is often advisable to glue it on wooden or pressboard bases. (Premounted linoleum blocks can be purchased at art stores.) The thicker, "battleship" type of linoleum is more satisfactory to work with, but it is often difficult to find.

Although you can use any printing surface that meets your needs — anything you make, buy, or find — there are certain basic facts to remember:

1. If you want to print solid tones, the surface must be very smooth (sandpaper will help achieve such a surface).

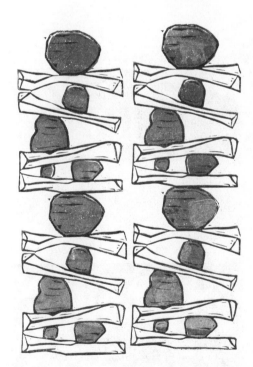

FIGURE 28 Linoleum block pattern.

FIGURE 32   Plank wood impression.

FIGURE 29   Pattern made with wood block (end grain).

FIGURE 30   Feather impression.

FIGURE 33   Carved wallpaper roller.

FIGURE 34   Indian wood block.

FIGURE 31   Cut gum erasers.

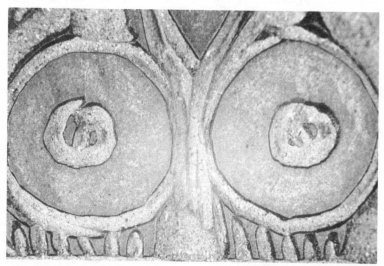

FIGURE 35   Cut linoleum.

2. The surface must be able to "hold" the smallest cuts you want to make.

3. Don't be afraid to use surfaces, such as wood, that have an interesting surface character of their own.

If you want to cut a design into the printing surface rather than use the uncut surface, you must usually draw cutting guidelines. White shoe polish will provide a surface on which to draw. Either draw directly on the white surface with pencil and then go over the design with India ink; or draw on paper with a soft pencil (5B) and transfer the design to the printing surface. Transfer the design by laying it face down on the block and burnishing (rubbing) the back with a smooth spoon or bone burnisher.

CUTTING TOOLS AND CUTTING

The tools you use will depend on what will best cut the printing surface you have chosen, as well as on your design and the types of cuts that it requires. You can almost cut a rough design in a gum eraser with your fingernail. On the other hand, for cutting end-grain boxwood you will need the traditional engraver's tools. For some textures, you don't need to cut at all; instead, you can bruise, hammer, or puncture the surface. If you like a certain surface texture as it is, leave it alone (if it will print). Cutting is not essential for obtaining an interesting surface.

All these possibilities are suggested in order to indicate that you must think for yourself and experiment. Find out how materials and methods fit together. In pattern work this is often done when you decide to elaborate on a sketched pattern. At this stage, you may choose a printing surface, tools, paper, colors, textures, and so on. A sketch can help you to plan your materials. Gradually you will develop the working habits and combinations that are right for you.

For a cutting tool, you can start with a jackknife. Wrap the smallest blade with masking tape or adhesive tape, as shown in Figure 36. An Exacto knife is even better. You will also need a small U-gouge to clear away the areas you don't want to print (Figure 36). More elaborate tools are unnecessary for cutting gum erasers, but they are needed for linoleum or wood.

A veiner (Figures 37 and 38) is also a very handy tool to have. Buy one or make it yourself from a gallon jug cork, a steel umbrella rib, and some spackle or crack filler. Cut a four-inch length of rib and use a file to shape one end rough-

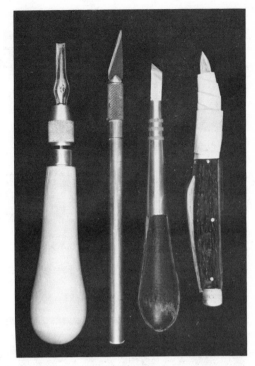

FIGURE 36 A U-gouge, an Exacto knife, a wood-cutting knife, and a wrapped jackknife.

FIGURE 37 Veiner and engraver's tool.

FIGURE 38 Cutting with a veiner.

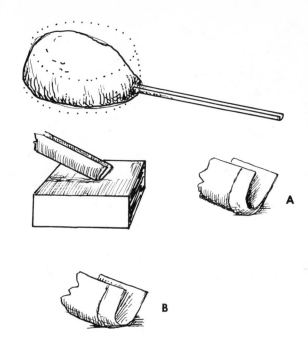

FIGURE 39 How to make and sharpen a veiner.

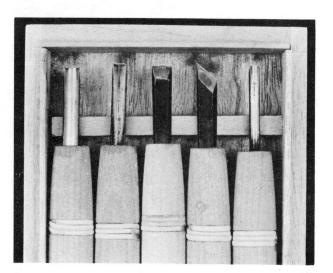

FIGURE 40 Japanese knife and woodcutter's tools.

FIGURE 41 Japanese method of cutting.

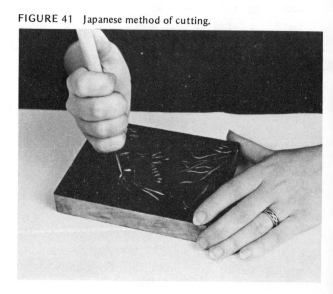

ly, as shown in Figure 39A. Next shape the end, as shown in Figure 39B, with an oilstone. You'll need medium-fine Arkansas oilstone (available at any hardware store) to keep all your cutting tools sharp. Shape the cork handle and cut a jagged hole in the bottom for the umbrella rib. Fill it with crack filler and before it sets, insert the rib as in Figure 39. After the crack filler has hardened, temper the steel tip by putting it in a gas flame until it is straw-colored, and then cool it immediately with water. Finally sharpen the tip on the oilstone, using shallow circular motions that will sharpen all parts of the U-shaped cutting edge evenly.

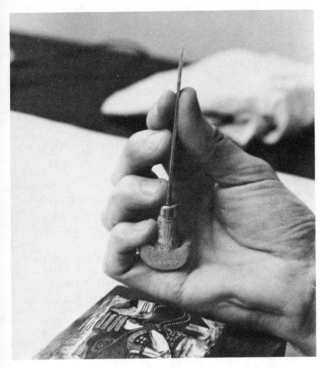

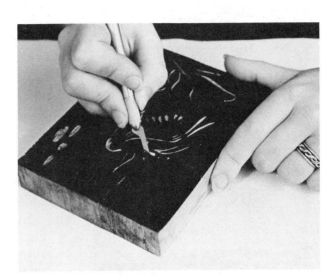

FIGURE 43 Cutting a wood block.

FIGURE 42 Using an engraver.

You can buy sets of linoleum-cutting, woodcutting, or wood-engraving tools (Figure 40). These are made to be used in several different ways, some of which are described with the products. A Japanese method of using the cutting knife is shown in Figure 41, and the method of using the traditional wood engraver's tool is shown in Figure 42. Choose the method you prefer — the one that gives you the best control.

The purpose of cutting is to clear away the parts of the printing surface that you do *not* want to print. Your cuts should slant toward the area that you are taking out of the surface (Figure 43). Try not to undercut the part of the surface that will remain. Never cut toward your hand. Take care not to lose control and thus cut into a line or area that you do not want to cut. This can happen easily if the material you are cutting is hard.

A design can be executed by cutting away only a few lines or small areas and allowing most of the surface to print; or most of the surface can be cut away allowing only a small amount to stand and print. The first method is referred to as "white line," because the lines often seem white. The second method is often called "black line." Obviously these two methods can be combined in the same design (Figure 44). The white-line work is easier to cut but harder to print because much more pressure is required to print large areas of ink than is needed for small areas. The black-line method is harder to cut but easier to print.

FIGURE 44 Black- and white-line work.

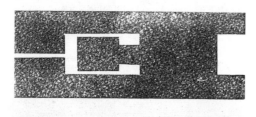

FIGURE 45 Fine lines on smooth and rough paper.

FIGURE 46 Solid areas printed on watercolor paper and newsprint.

SURFACES ON WHICH TO PRINT

Paper

Paper is by far the easiest and the cheapest surface on which to print, and it is available in many forms. Some of the easiest paper to print on, such as newsprint, is also the cheapest. By "easy to print on" we mean that the ink will transfer to the surface and print cleanly and completely, making it possible to print both solid areas and fine lines with minimum difficulty.

Fine lines that are filled in by too much ink, and solid areas that do not print completely, cause the most trouble in printing. Both of these problems can be magnified by using unsuitable papers which are rough-surfaced or hard-sized (Figure 45). Avoid nonabsorbent papers, such as bonds, that have been filled with glues or other material to make them smooth or nonabsorbent to inks. Usually a fairly soft, smooth, less-sized paper is preferable for patterns or prints.

If you want to print on a rough surface, you will have to accept some design limitations and make a bold design without fine lines or large, solid printing areas.

It is much easier to print on rough paper (in fact any paper) if it has been dampened. Pressing the paper for a few hours between damp blotters will dampen it. Even breathing on dry paper will make a difference.

Some very good and expensive papers are quite unsuited to block printing. For example, most watercolor papers are likely to be both rough and hard-sized (Figure 46). Although newsprint is cheap and easy to print on, it is made to last only a short time; it quickly becomes brittle and discolored. For a careful job you will need a better paper. Look for a paper you would like to use as a basic paper; but before buying in quantity, make tests, using your printing method. It may be worthwhile to investigate the heavier weights of "antique" book papers at a local printer. Another possible choice might be printer's cover stocks, which come in many colors and textures, although they are often rather hard-sized and must be dampened before printing.

Paper may have to be pasted, folded, or subjected to rather hard use. To protect it from paste, stains, and dirt, spray the finished design (before any pasting is done) with a protective plastic coating.

Cloth

Although cloth is tougher, more flexible, and longer lasting than paper, it can also be more difficult to print on. Several of the same considerations that apply to paper apply to cloth. A fairly smooth, flexible cloth without sizing or filler prints best.

Cloth should be washed before printing to remove the sizing and filler. Otherwise, when you print, you will print partly on the filler which will later wash out taking with it a part of your design. Wash, iron, and cut cloth to size before printing. Remember, cloth, like paper, is much easier to print on when it is damp (Figure 47).

Before you buy any quantity of cloth, be sure to test it with the printing method you are planning to use. Plain cotton broadcloth and muslin are fine for many purposes and if you want to dye your fabric, these materials take simple home dyes such as Tintex and Rit very well.

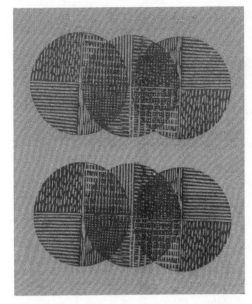

FIGURE 47 Printing on cloth — dry (top) and damp (bottom).

INKS AND DYES

Ink pads are fine for sketching, but they are very limited in size, range of color, and permanence. Poster colors brushed on bigger blocks give a much wider range of colors for printing on paper, and they are fairly permanent as long as the design is not subjected to much use, wear, or sun. Poster colors are not suitable, however, for printing on fabrics, and they dry too quickly for easy handling.

Some water-based inks are used in block printing and are available in tubes. They are rolled out with an ink roller or brayer (a rubber or composition roller). Although they can be cleaned up easily with water, they have the same limitations as the poster colors as far as durability and handling are concerned.

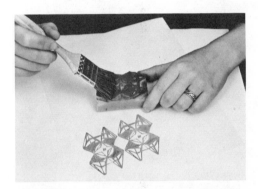

FIGURE 48 Brushing on water-based colors.

For more durable and permanent work, you will probably want to use oil-based inks (Figure 48). They are somewhat of a nuisance to clean up (use kerosene or benzine), but you will find them very flexible to use. The most satisfactory forms for the oil colors used in block printing are tubes of artists' colors and printers' inks (Figure 49). They can be obtained in a wide range of colors at art and printing supply stores. The printers' colors are generally cheaper and just as satisfactory as the artists'.

Start with the colors you like best, but don't forget white

FIGURE 49 Tools, brayers, and inks.

SIMPLE PRINTING METHODS

FIGURE 50   Mixing ink.

because you are likely to need more of it than any other ink. Use printers' white ink; artists' white is not suitable as a mixer. Red, blue, and yellow, the primary colors, can be mixed to produce other colors (Figure 50). Reds and blues make violets, reds and yellows make oranges, blues and yellows make greens. To get different shades, you can lighten these colors with white or darken them with black.

Colors are very strong when they come from the tube and usually they must be mixed with white, or with a transparent substance that printers call "extender." Extender is very useful because it lightens colors without the whitening effect of printers' white ink, and makes them easier to print. The extender or the printers' white ink should be used with both printers' inks and artists' colors. The artists' colors do not have sufficient body to use alone.

When you mix inks try to keep the mixture simple; when too many colors are mixed, the result is usually a muddy color. It is important to remember that the colors are strong, so start with extender or white and add the color to it rather than the other way around. Add the color a little at a time because a little goes a long way. Don't mix a great deal of ink for a small job. A half cubic inch is sufficient for most sketching purposes.

To print easily on most papers, oil ink should be about the consistency of toothpaste. If it needs to be thinned after it is mixed, use a few drops of boiled linseed oil. Don't make it too thin because you can only thicken it by adding color or white.

INKING: ROLLING AND DABBING

You can ink a printing block by pressing the block onto the ink supply (as with the stamp pad), by brushing on pigment (as with the poster colors), or by using a dabber or roller to apply the ink to the printing surface.

When oil inks were first used, they were applied with dabbers or leather "ink balls," as they were called; but today rubber or composition rollers (brayers) are used. If you are going to print with oil inks, you will want to get an ink roller in an art or printers' supply store; in fact it is handy to have more than one, in case you are printing more than one color at a time. Get the soft rubber or composition roller, not the hard one. Gum erasers make fine ink dabbers in an emergency.

With a brayer the ink is rolled onto a film on a flat, clean surface such as a sheet of glass (Figure 51). Usually a thin film is best, but "thin" is relative to the kind of design you are printing and the paper you are using. The best rule is to use as little ink as you can and still get your solid areas to print. Too much ink fills in the thin lines. The brayer, charged with the ink, is rolled over the surface of the block to be printed. Roll more than once, and be careful not to miss any spots. (When sketching, stamp the gum eraser on the rolled out film of ink.)

At times you may not want the ink to be evenly applied. You may prefer it uneven, unusually heavy, or unusually light, so that it does not print solidly. If so, apply the ink in the way you want it to print. You can graduate it when you roll it on (Figure 52) by going zigzag down a block without re-inking the brayer. Before printing, you can even mark the ink or texture it after it has been applied to the block. In handprinting there is no reason why every repeat or every copy of a print has to be exactly the same. The choice is up to you. You can use the edge of the brayer to make a rough line as was done in Plates 19 and 20; or the face of an old brayer may have an interesting texture of its own. Learn how to roll out an even tone of ink and print it. But then feel free to experiment.

FIGURE 51   Rolling out ink.

FIGURE 52   Gradated inking.

PRINTING THE IMAGE

So far we have described the steps that are preliminary to the actual printing process. The final step, of course, is transferring the image from the printing surface to the paper. This can be done in many different ways. The advantage of making patterns and prints in stages is that it allows decisions to be made at any point. The emphasis is therefore on creativity rather than on the production of many identical copies.

Stamping

As you know from working with potatoes and gum rubber, the simplest way to transfer the ink to the paper is to press the flat printing surface down on something like an ink pad and then down on the paper. When this is reversed, as it is in some printing methods, and the paper is pressed down onto the printing surface, the new printing elements cannot be

FIGURE 53   Use of the printing mallet.

registered accurately by eye. Some sort of mechanical registry has to be used. It is always preferable, especially in pattern development, to see what you are doing.

Printing Larger Blocks

With larger designs you will probably use linoleum backed with plywood or presswood, which is less likely to warp than natural wood. When printing with relief blocks, always print on a padded surface of some kind. Old newspapers make a fine padded surface. If you are printing a large surface such as drapery, it is easier to move your padding as you print rather than to put padding on the entire printing area.

Since you can't print large designs with the force of your arm alone as you did with the potato and the eraser, you may hit the block with a printing mallet (Figure 53) or tread (stand on) the block. For a printing mallet, any solid, padded weight or cheap rubber mallet is suitable. Just hit the block once — sharply. Avoid moving the block. If you decide to print by stepping on the block, just stand on it for a few seconds. Treading is an inaccurate term for it implies movement and you don't want the block to move at all.

Stencilling

Stencilling is the control of printing by masking off whatever areas you do not want to print. It allows a great deal of control and decision during printing and it can be a very useful process in pattern and print work, particularly when it is combined with other printing methods.

The printing area is masked off with stencil letters, cut oiled paper, wax paper, torn paper, cut plastic sheets, or actual objects. Held flat against the paper, the mask prevents the ink from printing the paper. By brush, dabber, sprayer, roller, or stamper, the ink is applied through the stencil directly onto the surface to be printed (Plates 19 and 20).

All the methods mentioned so far can be used with stencils, subject only to the limits of the stencilling process. With stencils of stencil paper, lightly oiled bond, or kitchen wax paper, you can print simple designs with a roller (Figure 54) or a gum eraser. If the stencil shape is larger than the roller or the eraser, interesting results can be obtained with several "hits" or rolls for each shape. You can also apply poster color directly through stencils with a brush or small foam-

FIGURE 54   Using a stencil with a roller.

rubber roller. Try to cut the corners of the stencil exactly. Cut a new one whenever you need it; or if you are using thin paper, cut several stencils at one time.

You will find it especially productive to experiment with a brayer and thin stencil paper (Figures 55 and 56). Combine the textures on the brayer with simple stencil shapes to create a delightful counterplay of semiaccidental images and shapes.

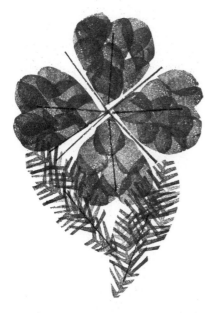

FIGURE 55   Two stencils built up by stamping.   FIGURE 56   Two stencils built up by rolling.

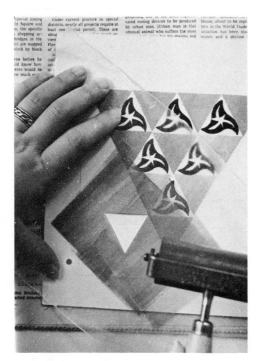

FIGURE 57 Stencil being registered.

With imaginative masking you can paint with brayer and stencil. As you do this, you obtain results that are nearly impossible to repeat, and the design becomes a unique print. In this process the brayer is used directly as a printing surface that carries a somewhat accidental image to the paper.

In pattern work, stencils are especially useful for the exact registry of geometric shapes and for printing flat colors, both of which are difficult to accomplish with relief-printing methods. Exact registry is obtained by looking down through the semitransparent stencil paper and seeing exactly how to position the design (Figure 57).

Understanding the principles behind the block printing and the stencilling processes will help you to experiment. Relief- or block-printing methods ink only where the block is placed. But stencil-printing methods ink anywhere the mask is **not** placed. The two processes are in many ways complementary and can be used together successfully (Figure 58).

Printing on Cloth

Printing and stencilling on cloth are almost entirely home crafts in this country although they are still practiced commercially in India and elsewhere. The commercial production of cloth in most countries is a highly mechanized technique dependent on very sophisticated dye chemistry. Printed fabrics produced with chemical dyes and chemical fixers (mordants) are too complex for most home use.

Special textile colors for home use, such as Versatex, are available for block printing and stencilling; but oil-based inks are the easiest to print on cloth and are therefore recommended here. Since printing on rough materials requires a thinner ink, use linseed oil as a thinning agent. Cloth also requires a softer surface to print on (more padding) and more pressure than is required by paper. A damp cloth under the cloth being printed is also helpful.

To increase the permanence of oil-base colors on a printed fabric, iron the fabric under a white cloth soaked in white vinegar before the ink is dry. Continue to iron until the pressing cloth is dry. The vinegar acts as a mordant to set the ink. For printed fabrics allow four to ten days drying time to permit the ink to set completely.

When printing block designs on cloth, mark pencil dots at the corners of the block each time you print. These dots

FIGURE 58 Combination stencil-and-relief design.

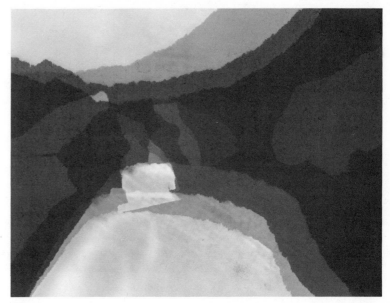

FIGURE 59 Photogram made with torn paper.

will serve as register guides. If the basic repeat unit is rectangular, keep the dots straight with the weave of the cloth. With other patterns, such as circles, such alignment is unnecessary.

Photographic Printing

The photographic process is essentially like stencilling. The light that acts as a printing agent similar to ink is partially obstructed or masked off from the final photographic print by the negative. Making photograms is a branch of photography that does not require a camera or negatives. Anything placed over the photographic paper when the paper is exposed to light masks off part or all of the light from some part of the paper and creates the image. If you have a friend with a darkroom, perhaps you can experiment with this form of stencilling. The photograms in Figures 59 and 60 were made with seedpods and torn paper.

With all these possibilities before us we are confronted with a question that faces professional artists as well as beginners: "What do I really want to do?" No one can answer

FIGURE 60 Photogram made with seedpods.

SIMPLE PRINTING METHODS

FIGURE 61   Printed shelf paper.

this for you. The best advice is simply to start out. Doodle a shape and work on it. If you want to make a pattern, try to cut the doodle into a shape you can repeat. Cut the doodle into an eraser and make a sketch. If you want to make a print instead of a pattern, you don't have to worry about repeating or sketching. Try it. Don't waste your enthusiasm by practicing too much. The methods suggested here make it possible to make your decisions one at a time and to see what you are doing as you go along. If your design reaches a stage where you don't like it, start again. Don't be afraid to copy something you like. William Blake, the artist and poet, said that copying was how he learned to be original.

PROJECT 2   PRINTED SHELF PAPER

Shelf-paper printing (Figure 61) is a very simple project to plan and to execute. The type of shelf paper that comes in rolls can be folded over to form an exposed edge or border that is perfect for printing. Look around the kitchen to get an idea for a design motif. It may be a kitchen utensil or part of a wallpaper design. Cut the design you have chosen into an eraser or potato, and ink it on a stamp pad. Before going ahead with final production, it is a good idea to print a rough trial copy to see how your design will look. Use a guideline, even for the sketch. If you are satisfied with the trial copy, draw a guideline on the shelf paper and print your design. Like any exposed paper surface, your shelf paper will last longer if you give it a protective spray coating after you have finished.

If you are working with poster colors or oil-base ink instead of a stamp pad, you can adjust your design by changing the color. Suppose, for example, you print a trial design and fine it is too bold or too vibrant for your kitchen. Before you alter the design to make it smaller or less heavy, try it in a lighter color ink (use diluted ink). Often just adding white to the color brings satisfactory results and eliminates the need to change the design. A strong or large design in a light color often has an impact similar to that of a small, delicate design in a darker, more aggressive color. Therefore, if the sketch of your border design looks too strong in red, try the same design in light blue or in a light shade of the color that is dominant in your kitchen.

PROJECT 3   PRINTED NECKTIE

Printing a pattern on a necktie is not difficult. Working out the design, however, is interesting because of the shape of the necktie and because you will have to print on a folded ready-made tie unless you want to make one yourself.

Buy a plain tie with no design in a color you like. The fabric should be a fairly smooth, close-textured cotton or synthetic, not a rough wool. Use oil-base inks and don't try to print solid areas because the folded tie will not provide a smooth enough surface.

Your design should be adaptable to the shape of the tie which is wider at some points than at others. The design in Figure 62 is an irregular scattering of red stars and blue bursts on a green acetate material. Oil inks were put on with gum erasers. Alternative solutions could be self-contained designs in the lower part of the tie, ink sprayed through a stencil, or monograms.

FIGURE 62   Printed necktie.

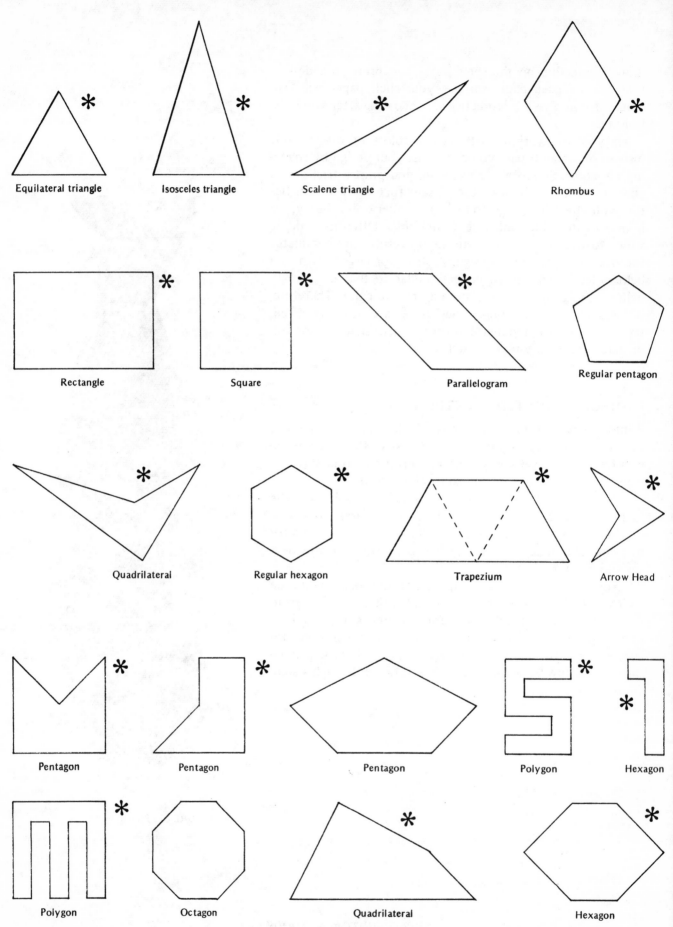

FIGURE 63 Geometric shapes.

3

BASIC FRAMEWORKS AND REPEATING SHAPES

You already know that some regular shapes, like rectangles and triangles, can cover an area with no gaps or overlaps; while some, like circles, cannot. Regular repeating shapes that can cover a plane surface are the frames into which pattern designs are placed. You have seen some effects they can have on design. It is worth investigating these frames or basic shapes further, not only because you can put designs into them, but also because they are often used as patterns themselves.

GEOMETRY OF REPEATING SHAPES

When the basic shapes are used as patterns, the results are often called tiling patterns, mosaics, or sometimes tessellations. These shapes have a mathematical beauty that you can learn to appreciate for yourself. Experiment with the geometric patterns — only a ruler, a compass, and a triangle are necessary.

Some of the common geometric shapes with which we will be working are shown in Figure 63. You are probably familiar with these figures, but a quick review might be helpful. The triangle has three sides. The equilateral triangle is a special triangle in which the sides are equal in length. The quadrilateral has four sides. The rectangle is a special quadrilateral that has four right angles (square corners), and the square is a special rectangle having four right angles and four equal sides. The pentagon has five sides, and the hexagon has six sides — but the sides and angles are not necessarily equal. If they are equal, the figure can be called a regular pentagon or regular hexagon.

TILING PATTERNS

If a surface is to be completely covered by a set of regular shapes — those with equal angles and equal sides — then the shapes can have only three, four, or six sides. On the other hand, there is no limit to the possible combinations of irregular figures that have unequal sides and angles.

Tiling patterns without gaps or overlaps can be formed from all the regular (equal sides and angles) figures shown in Figure 64, except the regular pentagon. The starred figures in Figure 63 can form tiling patterns, but those that are unstarred cannot. In other words, the starred shapes can cover an area without gaps or overlaps. They are, therefore, useful for repeating patterns which can consist of geometric shapes alone or of geometric shapes with designs, colors, and textures added.

It is easy to make use of these geometric shapes. Trace some of the starred shapes and see what patterns you can make by either stencilling with wax paper or stamping with cut gum erasers. Print alternate shapes (or all the shapes that are turned in one direction) one color. Several such solutions are illustrated in Figure 64. By working out similar solutions for yourself, you will discover how basic shapes can be used together and how they relate to each other.

Using simple printing methods to repeat shapes makes experimentation much more fascinating and enjoyable than using conventional drawing techniques, which can be quite tedious. One easy printing method is stamping a gum eraser over a wax paper stencil. Make the stencil by copying the basic shape from Figure 63 and cutting it from the wax paper. Cut several stencils at the same time before you begin to print and use a new one when necessary. Remember that good stencilling depends on keeping your brush or ink pad as dry as possible.

FIGURE 64   Repeating patterns using starred shapes from Figure 63.

PEGBOARD EXPERIMENTATION

Tiling patterns made from basic geometric shapes that cover a surface are the basic framework of pattern work. There may be one or more basic shapes in one pattern. They are the working and repeating units whether they actually appear in the pattern or not. Unfortunately, most pattern work doesn't take advantage of the variety of shapes available. Usually designs and color are varied within a small number of shapes such as the rectangle, parallelogram, and triangle. Nevertheless, there is a world of variety possible with just these few shapes, as you can see in most pattern work. But you can experiment with many other shapes by working with pegboards (Figure 65).

Make two pegboards, one in which the pegs (nails) form a square pattern and the other in which they form equilateral triangles. These are very basic shapes in pattern work.

FIGURE 65 Shapes on a pegboard.

To make and work with the pegboards, you will need the following:

A smooth board (not too hard) about a foot square or larger
Thin 1/2-inch nails
Black paint
Square graph paper
Triangular graph paper

Ruler
Compass
A 30-60-90-degree triangle
Pencil
2-inch elastics (2-3 dozen)
Hammer

The common one-inch square graph paper is readily available, but the triangular paper, which is called isometric paper, is more difficult to find. If you cannot find any, copy the sample in Figure 66.

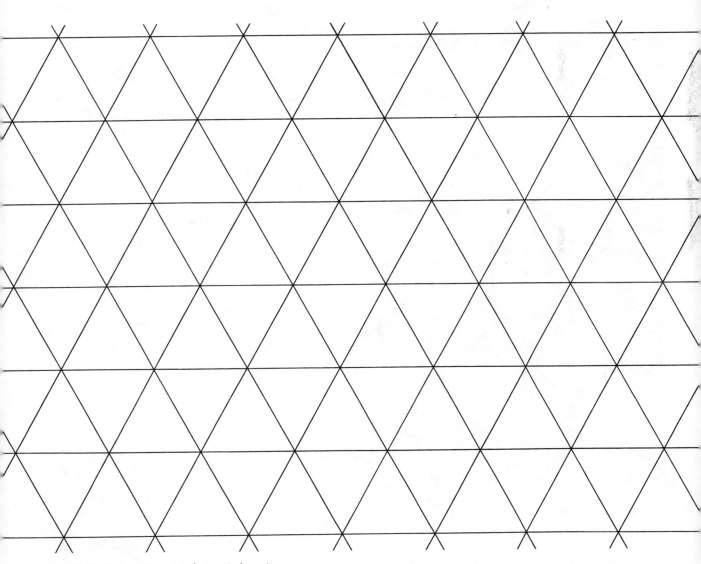

FIGURE 66   Model of isometric (triangular) graph paper.

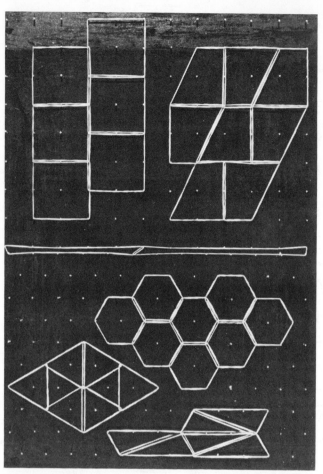

FIGURE 67   Pegboard with basic shapes outlined in elastics.

FIGURE 68   Pegboard patterns.

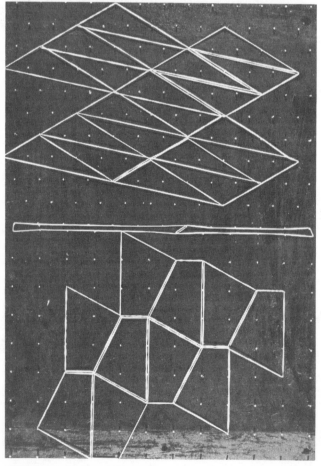

FIGURE 69   Pegboard patterns.

FIGURE 70   Pegboard with several repeats.

First you will have to make the pegboard itself, but it is worth the effort. Paint the board black and attach the graph paper to cover one side. In the illustrations both square and triangular patterns are inserted on the same board, but you may want to use two separate boards for the two configurations. Drive the nails through the graph paper into the board at the corners of the one-inch squares or triangles. Do not drive the nails all the way in, but allow them to stick up about ¼ inch. When all the nails are in position, rip off the graph paper and your pegboard is finished. Use it by stretching elastics around the nails to form the basic shapes as was done in Figure 67. If the elastics aren't long enough, you can use string; but the elastics are easier.

The pegboard is the easiest way to experiment with basic shapes and tiling patterns since you can judge the result by eye (Figures 68 and 69). First enclose a shape you like with an elastic, then see if you can repeat this shape to form a pattern. You can make many different shapes with the elastics, usually one elastic for each shape. When you get a repeating shape you like (Figure 70), transfer a section of the pattern to graph paper for easy reference (Figure 71). Then put a sheet of tracing paper over the graph paper and sketch in the colors, textures, or designs you may want in each basic shape (Figure 72). If you like simple geometric shapes, print them

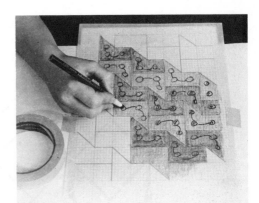

FIGURE 72 Experimenting with color and design over the graph-paper pattern in Figure 71.

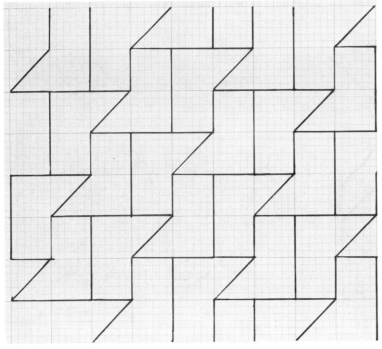

FIGURE 71 One of the patterns in Figure 70 transferred to graph paper.

FIGURE 73 Pegboard patterns with more than one basic shape.

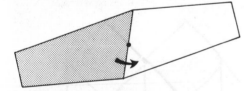

FIGURE 74 Rotated quadrilateral.

just as they are, perhaps using only a pattern of colors. Printing them by stencil is the easiest method, but remember that a plain geometric design, in which the edges must be sharp and join exactly, is most difficult to print because any imperfections are obvious.

One of the first things you learn when working with the pegboard is that many patterns are composed of more than one basic shape (Figure 73). Making such patterns is easier than explaining exactly how it is done. Look at the illustrations and work with the pegboard yourself. You will learn to make many pattern frameworks.

A tiling pattern can be formed from any triangle. Prove it to yourself on the pegboard. It is also true, but not so obvious, that a tiling pattern can be formed from any quadrilateral. This is done by turning the figure halfway, or 180 degrees around the middle point of any side (Figure 74). Make some irregular quadrilaterals on the pegboard or cut them out of cardboard. The illustrations will give you a start, but there is no end to the variations on the pegboard. It allows you to vary designs one step at a time, and to see just what you are doing.

Now that you know something about covering a surface without any gaps or overlaps, you can proceed to experiment with gaps and overlaps. When you get a basic geometric pattern, you can do anything you want with it. The pattern of irregular pentagons in Figure 75 has gaps that are parallelograms.

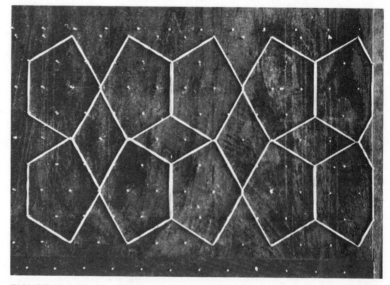

FIGURE 75 A pattern of irregular pentagons.

When you have made a pattern by repeating one basic shape or more, you will find that it is simple to modify this basic shape. Any modification will change the pattern and the way it works. For example, eliminate a corner or stretch one side in or out to a neighboring peg. Be sure to make the same modification in each shape in the pattern. Figure 76 illustrates a simple modification of Figure 75.

Another way to modify shapes is to add a new shape inside each original shape. You can add a new shape to every other shape or you can add one shape across two shapes (you are in effect adding a part of it to each of the two original shapes). Figures 77 through 80 show how this method can allow a simple set of basic shapes to grow into a complex design that you can control completely and easily. Remember to do the same thing to each set of basic shapes so that the design will remain a repeating pattern (Figure 81). You can also make unique patterns in which you vary the shapes in any way you wish. Sometimes you make a unique design and then see that with a small modification, it can be made into a repeat. In other words, you make a print and then find that you can put it into a basic shape and repeat it. A sure way of making a repeat from a unique design is to allow white space around the design by centering it in a basic repeat shape.

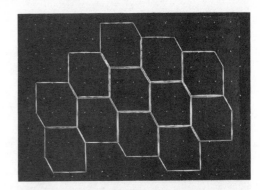

FIGURE 77   A pattern of basic shapes.

FIGURE 78   Addition of a new shape inside each shape of Figure 77.

FIGURE 76   Modification of a pattern of irregular pentagons.

FIGURE 79   Pattern modifications.

FIGURE 80   Pattern modifications.

BASIC FRAMEWORKS AND REPEATING SHAPES

FIGURE 81   Four pegboard repeating patterns.

4

PATTERN VARIATION TECHNIQUES

There are four things you can do to a design unit while retaining the same design and keeping it on a flat surface. You can move it around without turning it; you can turn it; you can make a mirror image or reflection of it; or you can make it larger or smaller. The negative forms of both the original and its mirror image are also usually considered to be the "same design." But that's all you can do without changing the actual design itself.

DROPS AND OTHER GRID MODIFICATIONS

By changing the position of a repeated shape, you do not change the basic shape itself; but you do change its relationship to the rest of the design (Plates 4 and 5). For example, if you cut several rows of square graph paper, you can make the brick pattern shown in Figure 82. If you cut several rows of triangular paper, you can combine the triangles to look like a wavy bar, as in Figure 83. This wavy-bar effect is called a chevron pattern. Both the brick and the chevron are common pattern designs.

If you turn the brick pattern to one side, it forms the half-drop pattern. Each adjacent row is dropped half of the

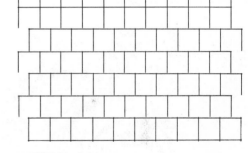

FIGURE 82 Brick pattern.

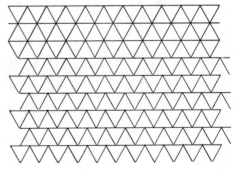

FIGURE 83 Chevron pattern.

FIGURE 84   Half-drop pattern.

basic unit in relation to the row next to it (Figure 84). Slide graph paper up and down and you will see that the drop need not be exactly one half of the basic unit. The half drop does, however, have a stability that other drops lack; smaller drops make the overall design seem to slide down while larger drops tend to make it climb.

The chevron pattern is the half-drop pattern done in equilateral triangles. In fact, any design or grid that has rows can be treated in a half-drop way, sliding the rows half a unit in relation to each other. It is often useful to find out how a checkerboard design will look in a half-drop form (Figure 85); sometimes it is a pleasant surprise. You will notice that the way the rows join or relate to each other changes, and these changes are very significant in the way the pattern looks. Do some experimenting with bricks and half drops of rectangles, using designs cut in gum rubber. Arrange the design so that it runs off the edge of the basic shape. Print it as a half drop and also as a checkerboard, observing the way the basic units join in each case (Figure 85). This joining is a very important aspect of pattern design because it is one of the principal ways in which the whole pattern is tied together (see page 44).

FIGURE 85   The same basic pattern is arranged in checkerboard (left) and half-drop (right) relationships.

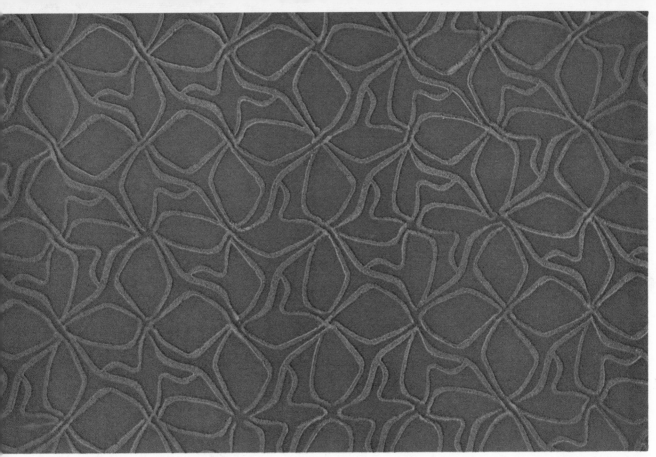

Plate 1   A design was cut on a square of gum-rubber eraser and printed on red cloth.

Plate 2   The pattern unit is from an Arapaho Indian design.

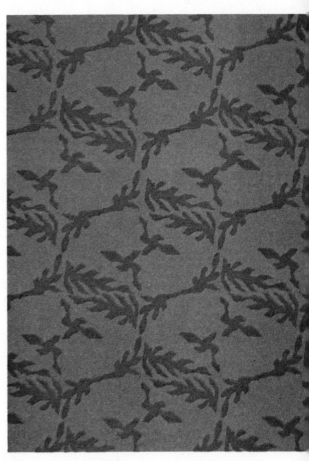

Plate 3   One square of gum eraser is rotated in a regular manner.

FIGURE 86   Rotation of the E shape.

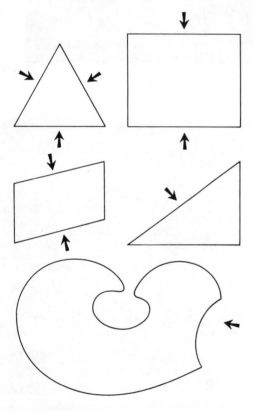

FIGURE 87   Any shape can be rotated in its own plane. Here the arrows show the number of times each shape looks the same in one rotation.

ROTATION

Turning the image, or rotation, is a very important way to vary a pattern (Plate 3). The different positions of the E shape in Figure 86 illustrate the meaning of rotation. If you turn the E shape in one full circle, or rotation, there is no position in which it looks the same. In other words, if you start in one position and turn the E, it will not look as it did in the starting position at any point in the rotation. This is not true of all shapes; for example, a circle will look the same as it does in the starting position in all phases of a complete rotation.

Turn this book in a full circle while looking at the equilateral triangle in Figure 87. For any starting position taken as position one, there will be two additional positions in which the triangle looks the same as it did in position one. The rectangle and parallelogram in Figure 87 look the same as they did in position one in only one additional position. Triangles with unequal sides and angles look the same in no other position than position one. A square with equal sides and equal angles has four positions in which it looks the same during a complete rotation. In fact any regular figure (with equal sides and equal angles) will have as many positions in which it looks the same as it has sides. In how many positions does a regular hexagon look the same? Most designs, however, are irregular and have no position during a rotation in which they look the same as they did in position one.

The rotation of any element can greatly affect elements around it, as shown in Figure 88. By itself the E has no position that resembles position one. But when two E units are combined in various ways, notice what happens. Of the four double figures shown, A and D have two "look-alike" positions while B and C have only one (the starting position). It is interesting that there are actually sixteen different ways that the two E figures in squares can face each other, but only one way that two solid squares can face each other. These sixteen different configurations are illustrated in the top two squares of each of the four-square figures in Figure 89. The two top squares are the only ones that turn, and they turn in an orderly way. The top left square turns completely around once before the top right square moves once (this is shown in the diagrams at the right).

Only sixteen configurations of the four-unit figures are shown since we have not turned the bottom two squares at all; actually there are 256 different ways in which the four E shapes can face each other. You can see, then, what great variety rotation can produce, at least with figures that have only one or two look-alike positions.

It is important that you learn to experiment with rotation in systematic ways similar to those used in Figure 89, because random rotating usually doesn't work very well. For instance, who would suspect from random observations that there are 256 ways in which four square E figures can face each other?

Cut half of a square eraser on the diagonal. If you turn this one element in systematic ways as you sketch on graph paper, you can experiment with some of the variety possible

FIGURE 88   Four combined E figures.

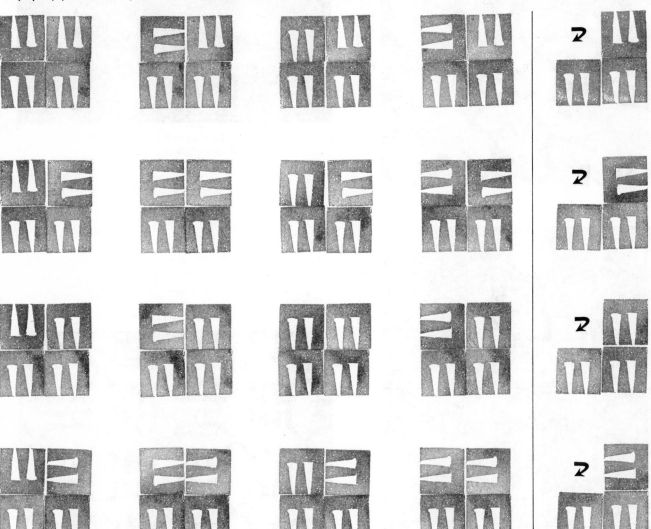

FIGURE 89   Sixteen different combinations of four-unit squares.

Plate 4   A rotated single square looks like a half-drop
          pattern.

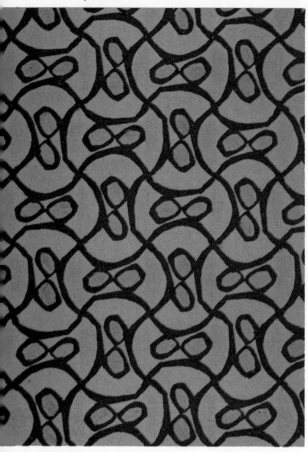

Plate 5   A double square basic unit is used for the flower, and an
          actual half drop is employed.

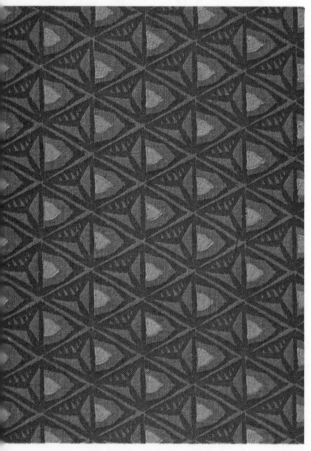

Plate 6   Pattern in which the triangle is cut from one
          square, and the white is added later.

Plate 7   Rotation is combined with corners that join.

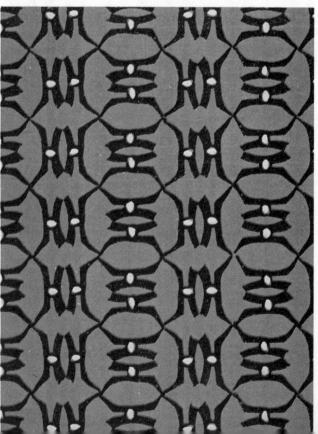

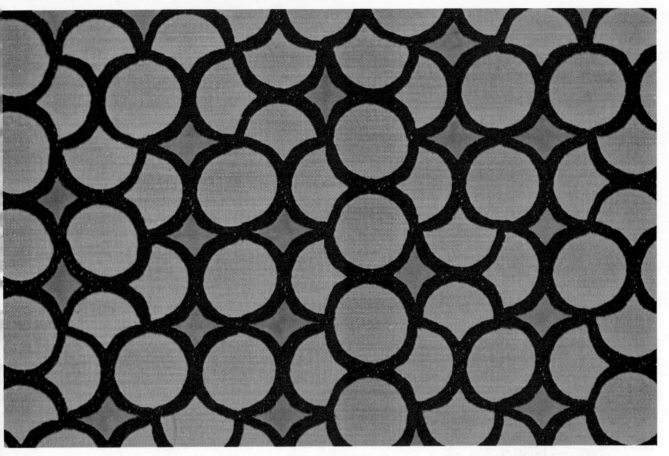

Plate 8   Random rotation with corners that join produce a variety of shapes. Similar shapes can be colored to produce various effects.

Plate 9   One design, in a square shape, is rotated.

Plate 10   Two circle designs complement each other in a simple but
           striking way.

FIGURE 90 Pattern made by rotating one quarter of the design.

FIGURE 91 A design made with an Indian cotton printer's block. The shaded area shows the size of the smallest design unit.

just through rotation. Look at Figure 90 in which one quarter or corner of the whole pattern was designed and then that quarter itself rotated. Try something similar yourself.

JOINING AND MATCHING

When designs extend to the edge of the basic unit on which they are planned, they seem to join with the neighboring designs. The joining of designs is affected by several factors: how the design is planned in the basic shape; how it is varied (by half drops or rotation, for example); and how many times the design "looks alike" in one rotation. Once you decide on the basic unit and its treatment, you can then plan the joins. Experiment on paper, step by step.

The planning of joins and matches is perhaps the most mysterious part of pattern design. A shape should not only make a join with its neighbor, but it should also make joins that are satisfying when repeated many times in the finished pattern (Plate 7). The complex design in Figure 91 was made with an Indian cotton printer's block. Indian designs are very subtle in their joining of basic units. By connecting any nearest four places in which the design is repeated exactly, you will find the smallest basic unit (but not necessarily the printing unit). The corners of the shaded area of Plate 7 are one set of four identical "nearest" points in that design.

The lines and angles in Figure 92 also demonstrate subtlety in the use of joins, but in a very different way. This pattern has one design (Figure 93) printed in a checkerboard and simply rotated in a random way. The design is one of a group that makes adequate joins, no matter how it is rotated. Another such design is shown in Figure 94. Like the first, it is simply sketched so that you can see the joins clearly. If it were mechanically produced, it might be difficult to see how it was planned, and what basic unit was used. Striking patterns can be made from designs such as these by rotating the basic unit only occasionally.

COUNTERCHANGE

A counterchange pattern is one that uses a design element in its negative or reverse image as well as in its positive or original form. It is as if both negative and positive photographic

FIGURE 92   Joins in a randomly rotated checkerboard design.

Plate 11   A pattern in which one shape is used in its mirror image and negative forms.

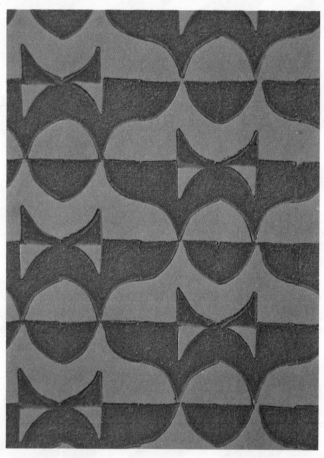

Plate 12   A double square unit is cut so that its joined shapes produce interlocking ovals.

Plate 13   A design sketch for a 3600-square-foot mural painting.

Plate 14   Tissue paper is folded into equilateral triangles. Before the paper was dyed, it was
dipped in water, which made the colors
soft at the edges.

Plate 15   The harder edges here result from
dyeing dry paper. The fold is triangular.

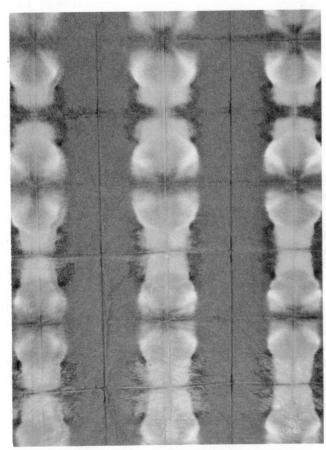

Plate 16   Rectangular folds can produce stripes, and the sides of a
shape can be dipped as well as corners.

FIGURE 93 One unit of the checkerboard design used in Figure 92.

FIGURE 94 U-pattern design created by random rotation.

FIGURE 95 A simple counterchange pattern.

images of the same design were used. The simplest counterchange is the checkerboard pattern in which each square is the "opposite" color of the square next to it. When the same shape in the same design is treated in three different colors, it is sometimes referred to as triple counterchange. In addition to color, some element of the actual design is usually treated in counterchange by reversing it. A simple counterchange is illustrated in Figure 95. Any grid pattern is suitable for this variation. All that is required is that at least one basic shape be treated in two or more opposing ways.

The easiest way to make a simple counterchange design is to draw and cut a positive and a negative of the design. If they are always to be printed in the same relationship to each other, then they can both be cut on the same block (Figure 96). Ordinarily a fairly bold design with strong solid areas works well. If the design is too complicated to draw freehand in the negative, make a heavily inked print of the positive version. Transfer the design to an uncut block of the same size by attaching the print face down on the block and burnishing the back. The image will transfer to the block and you can cut those parts of the design that were *not* cut in the positive version.

FIGURE 96 A counterchange pattern cut on one block.

REFLECTION

Mirror-image reflection is one of the four basic ways in which designs on a plane surface are varied without actually changing the designs. Many shapes are naturally symmetrical in that one half looks like the mirror image of the other half. A leaf is roughly symmetrical in this sense.

Reflection can be combined with counterchange and rotation to provide an infinite number of pattern variations. The leaf design in Figure 97 illustrates the combination of reflection and counterchange. The top portion is the counterchanged mirror image or reflection of the bottom portion. Study the pattern in Figure 97 and you will quickly get the idea. This technique can be used with abstract subjects or subjects that have no natural symmetry because any object you can see can have a mirror image, too.

FIGURE 97 Reflection and counterchange combined in a leaf design.

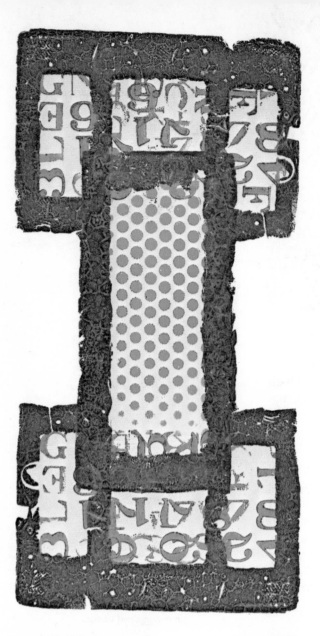

Plate 17   A relief print made with pieces of styrofoam, rubber toy letters, and perforated plastic sheeting printed through by the roller.

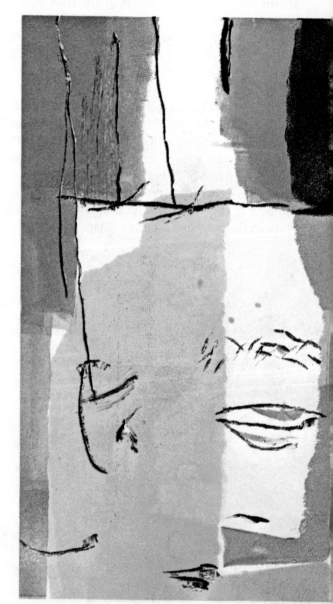

Plate 18   An "offset" print made with the roller, masking only the edges of the print.

Plate 19

Plate 20

The prints in Plates 19 and 20 are made with the roller, with wax paper used for masking. The edge of the roller is used to make lines.

FIGURE 98 One-eighth of image of pattern in Figure 90 reflected in a mirror.

FIGURE 99 Computer patterns. One octant is marked.

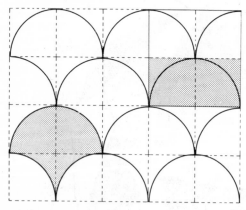

FIGURE 100 Scale design.

If you look at a variety of pattern work you will see that reflection and counterchange are common, both separately and in combination (Plates 11 and 13). Probably one of the most natural patternmaking experiments is to contrast a design with some dramatic modification of itself. This is a very useful procedure because it introduces both variety and unity into the pattern.

Figure 98 is one half of each quarter of the pattern in Figure 90. Its reflection in the mirror completes the quarter of the whole pattern. The whole pattern, as we have seen, results from rotating this one quarter. Rotation and reflection can introduce dramatic pattern modifications. An excellent example is the toy kaleidoscope. The kaleidoscope contains a random assortment of pieces of colored glass. By reflection in a set of mirrors, an infinite number of patterns are created from these pieces. In Figure 99 a computer has followed a similar procedure. The computer uses a random collection of dots in the octant (half of one quarter) marked. It then makes the other half of the quarter by a technique similar to reflection or mirror imagery. The computer then rotates the design of the quarter three times to form the square.

CURVES

Most of the basic shapes we have considered so far have contained only straight line segments. We have concentrated on the basic shapes that can be made from squares and equilateral triangles on the pegboard. But what can be done if some of the straight lines are modified into curves? One way to experiment with curves is to modify the straight lines of square and triangular graph paper, using a compass.

Since we want to *modify* the basic shapes rather than change them completely, the area of each basic unit must stay the same. If you subtract area from a basic unit in one place, you have to add it in another place. If you add a piece to a basic unit, you must subtract the same size piece from the same unit. All sorts of modifications are possible as long as you follow this rule of compensation for each change.

Try modifying a square with a compass as shown in Figure 100. The basic unit is two small squares. If you subtract the two top corners of the square, you must replace an equal amount of area somewhere else. When you do this, you get the scale design. Using the same principle of addition and subtraction in a different way, you can create another familiar shape, the ogee pattern (Figure 101). Both the scale and the ogee are modified squares. You can modify all basic shapes (Figures 102 and 103) by following the principle of addition and subtraction.

It is interesting to note that certain shapes such as the ogee have been popular throughout pattern history. When patternmakers find a popular basic shape, they tend to vary what is put into the shape rather than trying to vary the basic shape itself (Figure 104).

If you want to cut a design with curves, draw it first on graph paper with a ruler, a compass, and a soft pencil (5B). Then place the drawing face down on the printing surface — wood, linoleum, or eraser — and burnish the back of the paper to transfer the design. Before trying to cut the design, touch it up or go over it with India ink. After you cut the design itself, cut deeply around the outside curves so that you can see the edges of the design clearly enough to print in register. When printing irregular shapes, it is best to leave linoleum unblocked or to block it with a cardboard that can be cut with tin shears like the linoleum itself. Ink and register the block carefully and then use a blank block to hit with the mallet or to stand on.

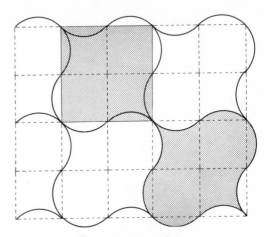

FIGURE 101   Ogee design.

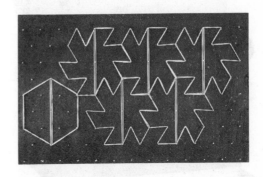

FIGURE 102   Three modifications of basic shapes.

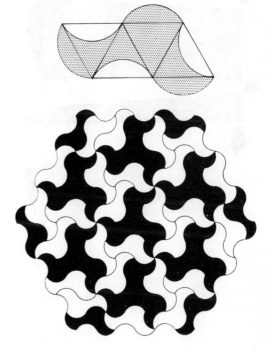

PATTERN VARIATION TECHNIQUES

Plate 21

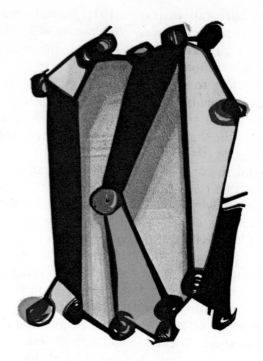

Plate 22

Plate 23

In these prints cut linoleum shapes are combined with roller printing through stencil shapes.

FIGURE 103 Example of an ogee pattern handprinted with one gum eraser.

FIGURE 104 Modified shapes.

POWDERING

Powdering means placing a design into a basic repeated shape and leaving ample space around it. Since the designs used are generally small, a great deal of the surface is often left unprinted. The principles for powdered repeats are the same as for all other repeats. The basic framework shape into which you place the small design need not be unusual since this framework is dropped; in addition the shape of the design itself does not necessarily bear any relationship to the shape of the repeat unit. Simple design motifs, such as the astrological sign of Taurus in Figure 105, are generally the best for powdered patterns. Monograms, alphabetic groups, or simply geometric doodles can also be used.

Powdered designs which have been in use since ancient times have a lasting charm. The Greeks often designed fabrics in a simple checkerboard pattern using a small geometric design in each checker (Figure 106). Then they either removed the grid, leaving a powdered effect, or left the checkerboard. The results were simple and elegant.

Powdered patterns are simple to design, but often tedious to print. If you plan to cover a considerable area with a small design put several repeats on one block.

FIGURE 105   Pattern made with the sign of Taurus.

FIGURE 106   Ancient Greek designs.

BORDERS AND CORNERS

Borders such as those on tablecloths, shelving paper, or pillowcases are basically stripes. A single stripe is a design that repeats only in one direction. Therefore, the basic repeat element needs to fit its neighbors on only two sides instead of on all sides as in a completely covered surface.

Borders have some other special properties that should also be considered. Although it may not be obvious, borders often have an inside and an outside, or a top and bottom. For example, the overhanging border of shelf paper has a top and bottom and a tablecloth border has an inside and an outside. One side of the border may be closed and the other side open (Figure 107). Sometimes this difference can be ignored, but sometimes it is built in purposely to lead the eye in one direction, for example, into the tablecloth. In symmetrical stripes each side of the design is the mirror image of the other (Figure 107).

Borders very often have to turn a corner, and making the join at the corner may be difficult unless you plan carefully. Two solutions are possible: make an even number of units on each side leaving one square unit on each corner to be filled in with a specially designed corner piece; or, for a square corner, mask off the printing of the last unit in each corner with a piece of scrap paper at a 45-degree angle (Figure 108). The first method involves more work than the second because it requires designing and printing a corner piece. Many designs can make attractive corners if masked in printing, but planning the join experimentally can usually improve it.

Borders are one of the easiest kinds of patterns to design and to print. They have all kinds of uses, from lace fringes on clothes to printers' ornamental borders for display work in books, pamphlets, and advertising. Some printers' borders are reproduced in Figure 109 to enable you to see how the problems of corners and symmetrical and unsymmetrical borders were solved.

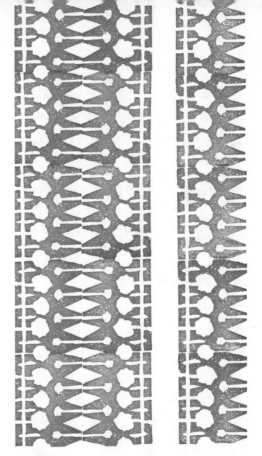

FIGURE 107   Open and closed border patterns.

FIGURE 108   Masking off the printing of a corner of a border.

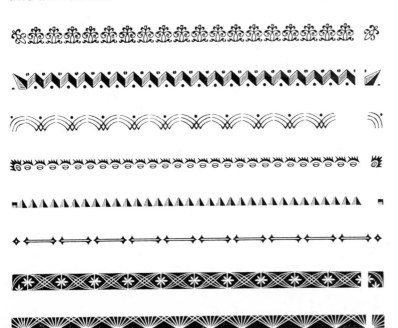

FIGURE 109   Printers' ornamental borders.

FIGURE 110   Stripe pattern marked and partially cut on a gum eraser.

FIGURE 111   Pattern made with the partially cut gum eraser in Figure 110.

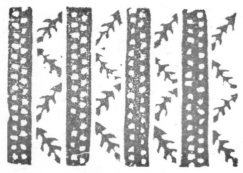

FIGURE 112   Pattern made with the completely cut gum eraser.

WORKING WITH STRIPES

The repetition of any basic unit in a row or line creates a stripe. The stripes on a checkerboard pattern run both horizontally and vertically, while the stripes on a half drop run in only one direction. A variety of designs can be created within these straight stripes.

Solid stripes are not easy to print perfectly by hand methods. Several basic units may have to be cut on one printing block. Doing so minimizes the labor of printing and also improves registry, since there are fewer units to be registered. Craftsmen such as Indian cloth printers always use as many repeats as possible on one printing block.

Figure 110 shows a 2 x 3 inch gum eraser marked and only partially cut in a stripe pattern. When the eraser is completely cut, it will contain a pattern of stripes of flowery sprigs and stripes that are solid except for some dots which make printing easier. Figure 110 shows only two completely cut stripes. The basic unit being repeated contains two sprigs (one pointing to the right and the other to the left) and a straight stripe. Although that unit could be cut and printed separately, it would be tedious and might cause registry errors. We have therefore chosen to cut eight such basic units on one gum eraser using the umbrella-rib veiner tool.

The printed pattern in Figure 111 shows the block in several stages of cutting. Sometimes you can finish part of the cutting completely before going ahead with the rest, as shown. Sometimes, however, it is better to cut each stage of the design roughly, without finishing any part completely, because you may change your mind and decide that the design will look best if you cut less than you had originally planned. You can't do that if you have already completed the cutting in one section. Allow the cutting tool to help develop the design; don't be too determined to produce just the pattern you had in mind when you started. The painter Georges Braque went so far as to say that any ideas he had before he actually started painting were invariably not usable.

Figure 112 shows a pattern made by the completed block and Figure 113 the printed design. You can see where the blocks are joined, but this is not objectionable and can even be regarded as part of the overall pattern. If you are printing a large area with stripes, however, it makes sense to use guidelines, especially for the first vertical row. It is usually true that getting a repeating design started accurately is the main problem, so draw a guideline, at least to start the first row and the first column.

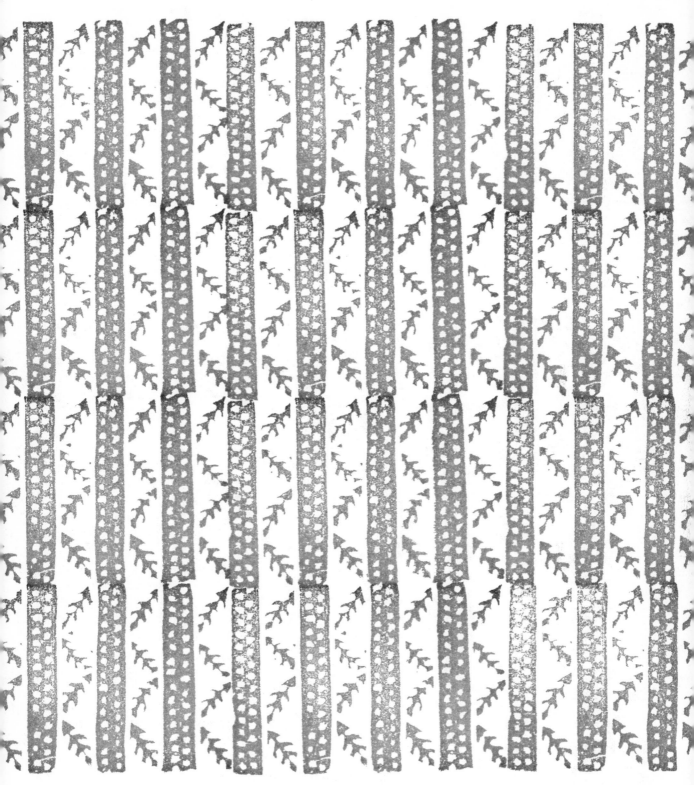

FIGURE 113   Repeated pattern made with the completely cut gum eraser.

FIGURE 114   Cut gum eraser.

CROSSED STRIPES

Repeating any basic unit in a row creates straight stripes, but putting designs into the basic units can create even more stripes (Figure 115). The horizontal and vertical stripes are most evident at first, but the diagonal ones also appear if you look for them. The eye goes from one set of pattern elements to another making it difficult to decide which is the real pattern. This ambiguity can be stimulating, as in modern "Op" (optical) art, which uses many such effects.

One of the pleasures of patternmaking is the power it affords for getting complex results by simple means. A pattern such as that in Figure 115 is more difficult to describe than to create, as you can see by looking at the cut block in Figure 114. If you look at the pattern you can tell that it could have been printed by using an entirely different printing unit.

FIGURE 115   Multistripe pattern made with cut gum eraser in Figure 114.

When we cross parallel stripes, new areas between the crossed lines are created. When the lines that cross are straight, various similar diamond shapes or checkerboards (Figure 116) are formed. If these shapes are filled in, textured, or colored in regular patterns, various designs emerge. Each small area is a basic parallelogram or rectangle. Patterns that are less regular, such as the one in Figure 117, can also be designed; this is a pattern based on crossed stripes and the regular pentagon.

Parallel sets of lines need not always be straight lines. They can be regularly bent lines (chevron style) or waved lines. When you cross two sets of bent lines at right angles, you get some interesting results in terms of the areas that the lines create. Figure 118 demonstrates how to experiment with two identical sets of lines, one on transparent paper moved about above the other. This is quite simple, but there are some tricks to it. If the sets are not at right angles or parallel, a unique rather than a repeating pattern will be the result. Also, if the distance between the parallel lines is not the same as the distance between the peaks in one line, the result will be more than one basic shape. The easy way to draw the parallel lines for use with this method is to draw them over graph paper. Each of the examples are composed of more than one basic shape. In Figure 119 the distance between the peaks is twice the distance between the parallels. This produces more than one basic shape, in this case two shapes and two reflections of those shapes.

Figures 120 and 121 show geometric designs which you may or may not like just as they are. They are like any other grid to which you can add color, texture, and shapes. When you get a grid you like by experimenting, put a piece of tracing paper over it and add colors or shapes.

FIGURE 116   Crossed parallel stripes.

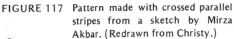

FIGURE 117   Pattern made with crossed parallel stripes from a sketch by Mirza Akbar. (Redrawn from Christy.)

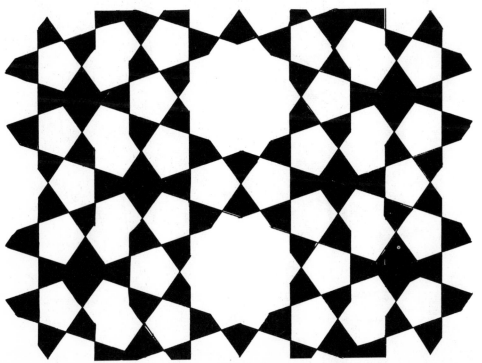

FIGURE 118

FIGURES 118-121 Parallel bent
and wavy lines.

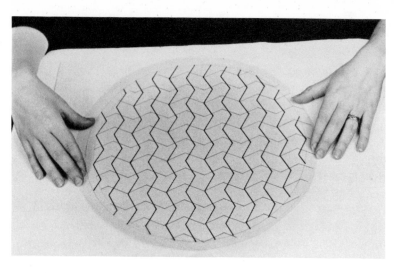

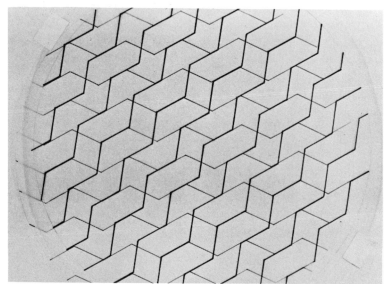

FIGURE 121

FIGURE 119

FIGURE 120

GETTING STARTED IN PRINTS AND PATTERNS

PROJECT 4 PRINTING A SCARF

A plain rectangular scarf, either made or bought, is perfect for pattern printing. Usually a lightweight decorative scarf is easier to print than the winter-muffler type because of the nature of the material.

The pattern can be an overall, a border, or a block design. As you plan the design, however, keep in mind that, although you will print the pattern on a flat rectangle, the scarf will be draped and folded when it is used. Any surface that is to be draped rather than used flat requires a design that can be appreciated when only partially seen. Avoid highly structured designs that can be understood only when viewed in their entirety.

The scarf in Figure 122 is light red orlon with a border of dark red designs that were printed with oil inks. In order to position the border design correctly, four strips of paper were printed and fitted together as a model that was visible through the material. Then the scarf was printed with the model as a guide. Notice that the border unit has an open design that does not require a corner piece.

FIGURE 122 Printed scarf.

PROJECT 5 WRAPPING-DISPENSER BOX COVER

If you'd like to have a decorative object in the kitchen rather than an advertisement, cover the wrapping paper dispenser for foil, wax paper, or Saran Wrap with a pattern. You needn't throw the box away when the wrapping is used up, just put a new supply of wrap into your box.

Most wrapping boxes are 2 inches wide and 12 or 12¼ inches long, a size that makes pattern planning simple. You will need one piece of paper to wrap around the box and two pieces for the ends (Figure 123). Don't forget to allow enough paper to cover the flap that is tucked in when the box is closed (Figure 124). Use a fairly heavy paper if there are plain areas in your design through which the advertising shows. Plan your design and print it, using the method you prefer.

Before you begin to paste the printed paper to the box, be sure it will fit exactly. You might experiment with plain paper to make sure the size is correct. Because the cutting edge must be left uncovered, it is probably easiest to start pasting just below it. If the cutting edge is on the bottom of the box rather than on the lip, cut your design to allow for

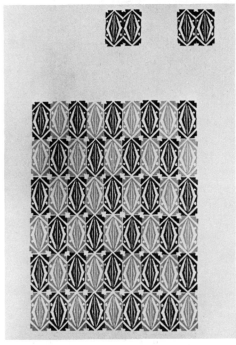

FIGURE 123 Pattern for covering wrapping-dispenser box.

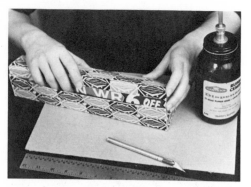

FIGURE 124 Covering a wrapping-dispenser box.

it. You may want the edges of your pattern to align at the corners of the box, at least along the top. This is sometimes difficult to arrange on all corners, but if you are very careful, you can do it. Of course, if your design is not linear in nature, this is not an important consideration.

Attach the covering securely to the box with rubber cement. Coat both the paper and the box and allow them to dry. Then mount the printed paper slowly. Coat the covering of the completed box with a protective plastic spray.

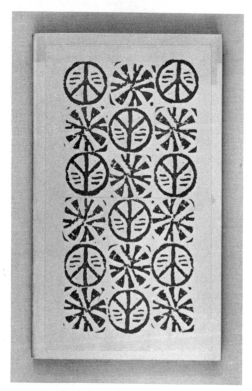

FIGURE 125 Book cover.

PROJECT 6 BOOK COVER

Books are frequently covered with patterned materials. Covering a book, however, can involve anything from completely rebinding it in tooled or stamped leather to adding the simplest ready-made plastic cover.

The cover in Figure 125 is made of red Con-Tact plastic with a blue-grey design. The checkerboard pattern was carefully planned ahead of time and fitted to the front panel of a paperback book cover. Oil inks were used and allowed to dry for several days.

The strong designs on the front covers of paperbacks will usually show through one layer of Con-Tact. This can be prevented by using two layers over the front and back panels. The extra layer can go either under or over the new cover for Con-Tact adheres very well to itself. If the extra layer goes over the new cover you can create a panel effect by using a contrasting color. In order to center the design accurately on the cover, it is sometimes preferable to print it after the cover is applied. The one advantage to having the original cover showing through is that you can letter the name of the book on the spine with acetate inks using the printed title as a lettering guide. If you make any lettering mistakes on the back, you can wash them off and start again.

To size the Con-Tact, lay the book on it and mark the dimensions of the front, spine, and back on the backing of the Con-Tact paper. Then add flaps as shown in Figure 126. Cut the plastic with the backing on it and lay it, backing side up, on a flat surface. Test the fit with the paper backing still attached. Then remove the backing and attach the paper to the spine. Attach the sides slowly from the spine out, trying not to make air bubbles (prick them with a pin if they form).

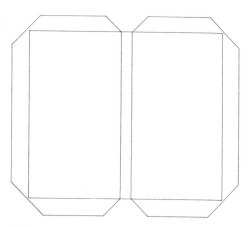

FIGURE 126 Diagram of pattern for book cover.

GETTING STARTED IN PRINTS AND PATTERNS

64

PROJECT 7 PENCIL HOLDER

A printed pattern wrapped around a tin can makes a decorative pencil holder. The holder will look neater if you plan the number of units in the design according to the height of the can, as in Figure 127, but this is not always necessary. It might be a good idea, too, to paint the can inside and out before applying the design. After planning and printing your design and sizing the paper, attach the printed pattern by coating both the can and the paper with rubber cement. Carefully roll the paper on keeping it as straight as possible (you can adjust it slightly by softening the rubber cement with benzine or lighter fluid). Spray the design with a plastic coating. You can also apply a design directly to the painted can with gum erasers and oil inks.

FIGURE 127 Printed pencil holder and stationery.

PROJECT 8 STATIONERY

Printing your own stationery (Figure 127) is fun and instructive as well. Although monograms (Figure 128) or private designs such as personal seals are not easy to design, they can be interesting and handsome. The Greeks were the inventors of the monogram, which is a sign composed of written characters interlaced with one another. Sometimes the letters are disguised or turned back to front. If they are simple, they can be cut in gum erasers. They can also be cut into the end of a wooden stick to make a handy printing stick. Remember that an engraving tool is usually necessary to cut end-grain wood.

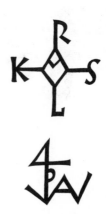

FIGURE 128 Monograms of Emperor Charlemagne and a man named Paul.

PROJECT 9 PATTERN-DYED GIFT-WRAP PAPERS

Decorated papers make very unique gift wrapping (Plates 14-16). They can be made with simple vegetable dyes, or household dyes (Rit or Tintex). Use highly absorbent papers, such as oriental rice paper, newsprint, or tissue paper. The technique is simple. First fold the paper into rectangles or triangles, as shown in Figure 129. Next dip the corners or edges of the folded paper into the coloring and press it out again almost immediately between folded newspapers or blotters. Unfold the paper carefully; extra care will be needed to unfold fragile tissue papers. Dry the papers flat and iron out the folds if you wish.

Experiment with different colors, and try wetting the

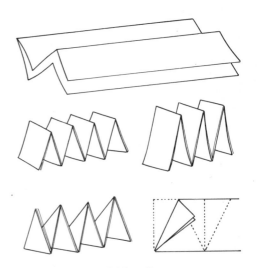

FIGURE 129 Paper-folding diagrams.

PATTERN VARIATION TECHNIQUES

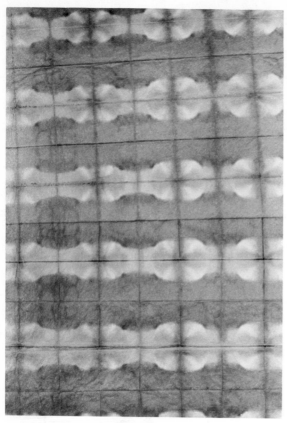

FIGURE 130   Gift-wrap paper.

FIGURE 131   Gift-wrap paper.

paper before dipping it into the dye. Since dye takes and spreads differently on wet paper, this technique produces an unusual effect (Figures 130 and 131). Papers dyed in this way can be the basis for additions of stencil- or block-printing designs.

OTHER TYPICAL PROJECTS

Aprons
Audio cassettes and reel boxes
Cannisters
Christmas decorations
Curtains and drapes
Decorative panels
Easter eggs
Handkerchiefs
Jewelry boxes
Lampshades
Manila envelopes

Napkins and tablecloth
Notebook covers
Patch pockets
Pillow covers
Placemats
Room dividers
Shopping bags
Splash-area covers
Toy chests
Window shades

5

PRINTS

UNIQUE PATTERNS

A print is usually a unique pattern (in which there is no repeat design), although almost anything that has been printed can be called a print. Historically an original print meant an artistic work made by the artist to be admired and perhaps framed.

In the past original prints were usually made by one of three important printing processes: relief printing, in which the areas to be printed are raised as in block printing; planographic printing, in which the areas that print and those that do not are on the same surface, and the pattern is offset; and intaglio printing, in which the areas that print are cut into the printing surface, ink is forced into them, and then drawn out again by pressing the surface hard against the paper. Traditionally these three main printing processes were used only one at a time. Today they are often used in combination with each other and with other processes such as blind stamping, stencilling, perforating, flocking, and monotype painting. Books on basic and combined methods are listed in the bibliography on page 83.

You can, however, make prints by using the graphic methods we have already covered. Study the prints in Plates

FIGURE 132   A print with a Mexican motif.

17 through 23. You need not be concerned about repeating patterns, despite the fact that you use basically the same printing methods. In some ways making unique prints is more difficult than making patterns, even though there are fewer guiding principles. In pattern work the mechanisms of repeating and the standard variation techniques do a great deal of design work for you. With unique prints that do not repeat, you're on your own.

NATURALISTIC DRAWING

Prints are often thought to be similar to paintings, but naturalistic drawing is not essential to printmaking. It is up to you. There are no rules; so if you want to draw naturalistically, you should do so. Drawing boldly is beneficial. Learn to experiment easily and to throw away what you don't like. The relatively easy printing methods given in this book will be helpful. Many artists do not draw naturalistically at all. In fact, modern printmakers are coming to the realization that unique prints can contain repeats and sometimes be very much like patterns.

Since each print is unique and individual, there is not as much you can learn from other people in printmaking as there is in patternmaking. Instead, look at modern and historical examples, such as those in Figures 132 and 133, to see the ways in which other people express themselves in prints. You will find there are similarities between the ways in which they work and what you have been doing in patternmaking. Any book on abstract art will give you a number of ideas that do not require drawing skills. Also use the step-by-step methods given in the first part of this book which enable you to see what you are doing and to make your decisions as you go along.

There are really no rules for designing unique prints, but the secret of the artist, James McNeill Whistler, might be helpful. He felt that much of the success of his etchings came from the fact that he worked on them from the center of interest outwards and whenever he felt the work looked well, he stopped. Usually he did not fill up the rectangle of the etching plate and the result was an unusual or vignetted shape. Try making some prints that grow from the center as well as from other directions.

Just as in pattern printing, it is important to see what you are doing while you work. But in making unique prints

FIGURE 133   Print by Hans Arp cut on plywood.

there is one possible exception to this rule. All the stages or printed impressions except the first should be done with the printing surface face down. The first stage can be done equally well with the printing surface up and the paper face down, but you can use this arrangement without losing control of your print because the first stage of a print does not need to register with or be compared to anything that went before it. You may therefore choose to put a great deal of your design into the first stage.

For those without printing presses, burnishing is the most useful method of printing a large relief block that is too big to print well by treading or using a mallet. Ink the block first and then lay the paper to be printed face down on it. Burnish the back of the paper with a large, smooth burnisher or spoon until the ink is sufficiently transferred to the paper (Figure 134). Damp paper, as usual, makes the printing easier and the result better. A sheet of hard paper between the spoon and the paper being printed helps to prevent damage to the print. Without shifting the paper you can lift the corners to see how the transfer of ink is progressing (Figure 135). When it is complete, you have a first-stage print. In the later stages, you can add stencil colors or patterns.

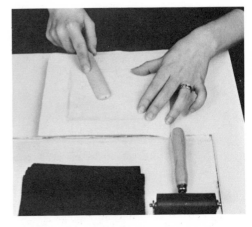

FIGURE 134   Burnishing.

FIGURE 135   Lifting the corner of the paper to check the ink transfer.

PRINTING PROCEDURES REVIEWED

A soft rubber brayer and kitchen wax paper together form a very flexible printing combination. Figure 136 shows a simple roller print made by rolling an inked brayer over pieces of paper that had been dropped on a glass surface covered with thin ink. The shapes stick to the brayer which is then rolled onto the paper, first one way and then back, after the shapes have been peeled off. You can see the shapes repeated. Each time you roll the roller, the ink becomes thinner producing some interesting shading.

FIGURE 136   Roller print.

Figure 137 shows the same technique used in a decorative way. A wax-paper stencil was used to mask the printing. After this was done several times, some small stencils and roller marks were used to accent the design. The roller and stencil have great potential as a team partly because you can texture the ink on the roller before you print through the stencil. For that matter, old rollers may have irregular textures of their own, so don't overlook the possibilities they offer.

FIGURE 137 Roller and stencil print.

If you want a formal type of work with hard edges and smooth colors instead of textures (Figures 138 and 139), you have to use a smooth roller. Roll the ink out and make clean cuts in the stencil paper. By using a brayer, you can't print an area that is any longer or wider than the outside surface of the brayer itself. The two designs illustrated are based on parts of two letters of the alphabet, A and D.

Don't be afraid to repeat your elements in different po-

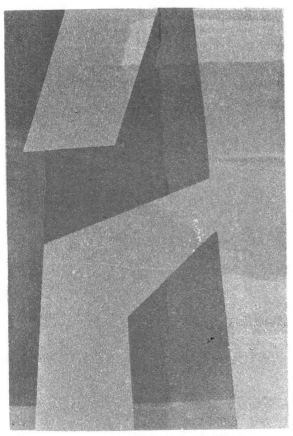

FIGURE 138 Stencil design based on part of the letter A.

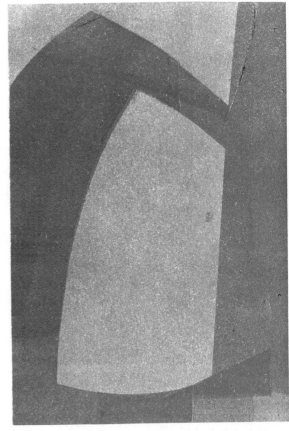

FIGURE 139 Stencil design based on part of the letter D.

sitions. As with pattern design, repetition with a difference gives a design both variety and unity (Figure 140). Just because your overall pattern is unique doesn't mean that you can't employ repeats. Use them and if you don't like the result, start again. The printing methods suggested are not difficult and they allow you much design freedom.

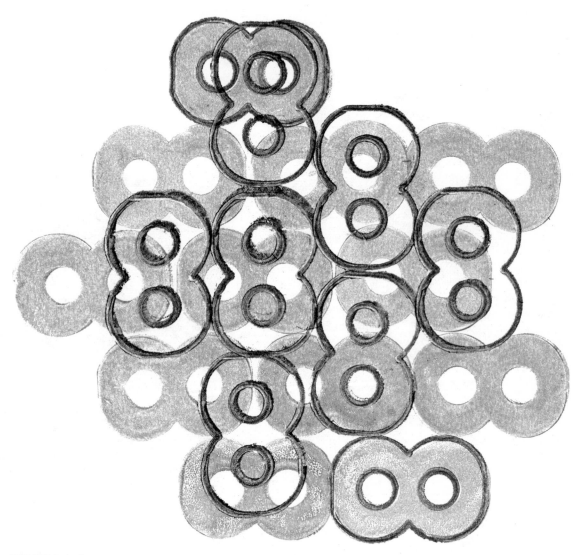

FIGURE 140   Pattern of 8's.

Mix the stencil technique with other methods, such as relief printing from letters, numerals, or found objects with interesting shapes and printable surfaces. You can use any object that will print — perforated plastic, waste styrofoam, old wood, rubber, etc. Figure 141 is an example of a print made from an electronic circuit.

FIGURE 142   Initial letter by Imre Reiner.

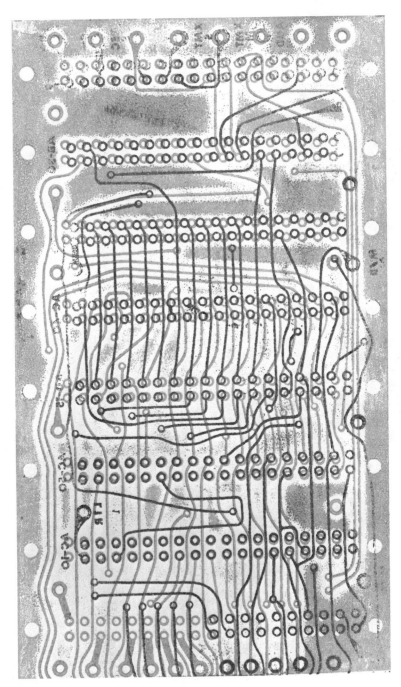

FIGURE 141   Electronic-circuit print.

By looking at the following examples you should get more of an idea of what can be done with the processes that have been described. Be individualistic and experiment widely. Most importantly, remember that *you* should be pleased with what you print. If you start worrying about pleasing others or being fashionable, you will miss most of the fun of creating your own prints.

FIGURE 143   Stencil with gum-eraser stamping.

FIGURE 144 Type metal scratched with a file.

FIGURE 145 Linoleum cut with stencilled color.

FIGURES 146 *(left)* and 147 *(above)* Stencil and roller prints.

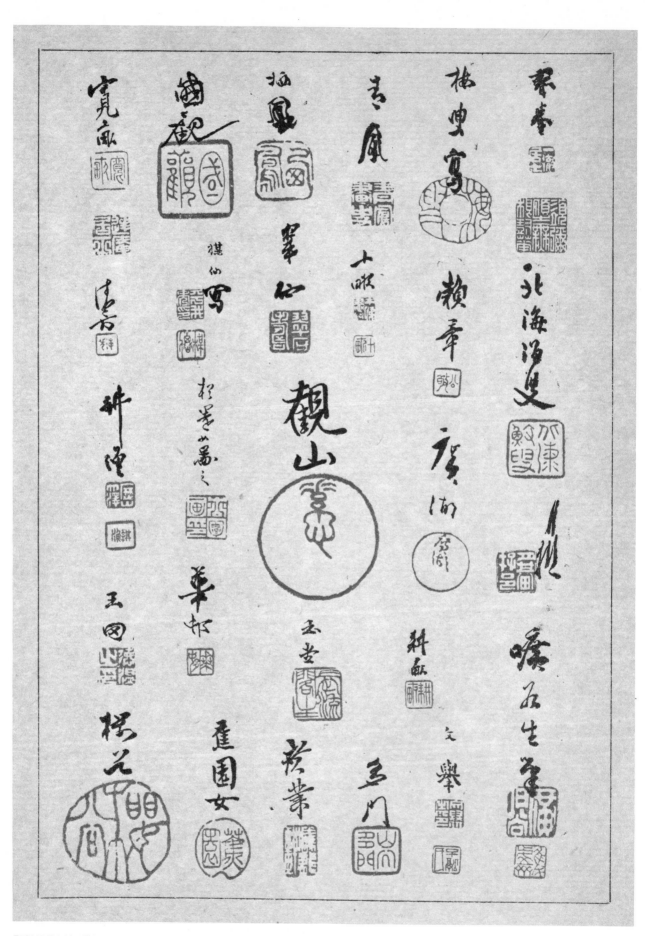

FIGURE 148　Signatures and seals of some contemporary Japanese artists.

FIGURE 149 *The Monkey Bridge, Hiroshige.* Japanese woodcut.

Courtesy of The Fogg Art Museum, Harvard University, Duel Collection

FIGURE 150 Wood engraving.

GLOSSARY

Black-line work — designs in which most of the printing surface of the printing block is cut away; only a small amount of the surface prints.

Block — usually a block of carved wood or linoleum with which to print. Any solid object used as a printing surface.

Block printing — usually, printing from wood or linoleum blocks.

Brayer — a roller used to ink a printing block.

Burnishing — rubbing; used in printing to mean rubbing the back of paper placed over a printing surface, to transfer the design.

Counterchange — the negative image of a design element used in combination with the positive form.

Dabber — a paint or ink applicator of rubber or cloth.

Design — the printing element that is put into the pattern framework.

Eraser and potato printing — two of the simplest printing methods that are used primarily for making sketches.

Gouge — a cutting tool for wood or linoleum used to remove large areas of material.

Joining — combining neighboring basic units in such a way as to form an additional feature of the overall design.

Negative — the reverse of an original design considered to be positive. The light areas become dark and the dark areas light.

Pattern framework — a formal structure, visible or invisible, into which a repeat design is placed.

Photogram — printing by using photographic stencilling techniques.

Powdering — placing a design in its framework so that ample space is left around the design itself.

Printing mallet — a hammer with a soft head used for hitting the back of the printing block.

Printing surface — surface used to transfer ink or paint to the paper or cloth.

Reflection — the mirror image of a design element.

Registering — having repeated designs in correct relationship to one another.

Registry mark — a mark used as an aid in aligning the design with those already printed.

Relief printing — printing with a printing surface that has a raised design.

Repeat — the printing unit that is repeated in a pattern.

Repeating pattern — a pattern that is composed of repeated units.

Rotation — turning a design unit around its central axis.

Sketch — rough, preliminary print of a design.

Stencilling — a process by which areas not to be printed are masked off.

Tiling pattern — a regular shape that covers a surface without gaps or overlaps.

Treading — printing the image by standing in place on the printing block.

Unique pattern — a print that does not have repeated units.

Veiner — a U-shaped cutting tool for wood or linoleum used for medium-fine detail work.

White-line work — designs produced by cutting away only a few lines or areas of the printing block; most of the surface is allowed to print.

BIBLIOGRAPHY

Batsford, Anthony Kinsey. *Introducing Screen Printing.* New York: Watson-Guptill Publications, 1967.

Bradley, A. Day. *The Geometry of Repeating Design.* New York: Columbia University Teachers College, 1930.

Christie, Archibald H. *Pattern Design.* Oxford at the Clarendon Press, 1930.

Cundy, H. M., and Rollett, A. P. *Mathematical Models,* 2d ed. Oxford at the Clarendon Press, 1951.

Day, Lewis F. *Pattern Design.* New York: Charles Scribner's Sons, 1903.

Dye, Daniel Sheets. *A Grammar of Chinese Lattice.* Cambridge, Mass.: Harvard University Press, 1937.

Edwards, Edward B. *Pattern and Design with Dynamic Symmetry.* New York: Dover Publications, 1967.

Entwhistle, E. A. *The Book of Wallpaper.* London: Arthur Barker Co., 1954.

Erickson, Janet. *Block Printing on Textiles.* New York: Watson-Guptill Publications, 1961.

Escher, M.C. *The Graphic Work of M. C. Escher.* New York: Meredith Press, 1967.

Fenn, Amor. *Abstract Design.* New York: Charles Scribner's Sons, 1930.

Gilmore, Pat. *Modern Prints.* New York: Studio Vista/ Dutton, 1970.

Gourdie, Tom. *Pattern Making for Schools.* London: Studio Publications, 1959.

Johnson, M. P., and Kaufman, G. *Design on Fabrics.* New York: Reinhold Pub. Corp., 1967.

Justema, William. *The Pleasures of Pattern.* New York: Reinhold Pub. Corp., 1968.

Kepes, Georgy, ed. *Module, Proportion, Symmetry, Rhythm.* New York: George Braziller, Inc., 1966.

MacMahon, P. A. *New Mathematical Pastimes.* Cambridge University Press.

Miles, Walter. *Designs for Craftsmen.* New York: Doubleday & Co., 1962.

Proctor, Richard M. *The Principles of Pattern.* New York: Van Nostrand Reinhold Co., 1969.

Proud, Nora. *Textile Printing and Dyeing.* New York: Reinhold Pub. Corp., 1965.

Rothenstein, Michael. *Frontiers of Print Making.* New York: Reinhold Pub. Corp., 1966.

Scherr-Thoss, S. P., and H. C. *Design and Color in Islamic Architecture.* Washington: Smithsonian Publication 4741, 1968.

Searle, V., and Clayson, R. *Screen Printing on Fabric.* New York: Watson-Guptill Publications, 1968.

Watson, John Forbes. *Collection of Specimens and Illustrations of the Textile Manufacturers of India.* London, 1873.

American Fabrics (Magazine)

INDEX